KILLER
PING-PONG

SURVIVING LIFE AT HOME

DAVID LAWRENCE

Scripture Union

This book is dedicated to Anna Williams, whose charm, wit and erudition make her a potential world champion player of **KILLER PING-PONG**

Other titles by David Lawrence:
The expanded Chocolate Teapot — *surviving at school*
The Superglue Sandwich — *for people who are stuck for an answer*
Travels with my Zebra — *making choices when everything is not black and white*

On Line with God — *practical help with how to pray*
Big Questions about God and You
Help! My Parents are Aliens — *more help for coping at home*

Text © David Lawrence, 2001
Illustrations © Taffy Davies, 2001

First published 2001

Scripture Union, 207–209 Queensway, Bletchley, MK2 2EB, England.

Killer Ping-Pong is a revised edition of the book Home but not Alone previously published by HarperCollins 1994.
ISBN 1 85999 468 7

British Library Cataloguing-in-Publication Data
A catalogue record for this book is available from the British Library.

Printed and bound in Great Britain by Cox & Wyman Ltd, Reading, Berks.

KILLER PING-PONG
(an unusually popular family game)

RULES

1 *KILLER PING-PONG* is a two-player game that you can play with one (or for more advanced players, both) of your parents.

2 All players should be in the same room. The smaller the room, the more intense the game. (Playing Travel *KILLER PING-PONG* on a long car journey is especially effective.)

3 To start the game your parent must ask you a question that you do not wish to answer truthfully, eg 'Where were you last night?' 'Have you done your homework?' 'Where is your school report?' etc etc.

4 You must then reply, using one of three permitted 'response tracks'. Assuming the opening question was, 'Where were you last night?' the answer must either be:
a) far-fetched, eg 'I was mowing the moon with my mates.'
b) vague, eg 'Nowhere much. I was just "out".'
c) off the subject, eg 'You look great this morning, Mum.'

5 Your parent must now put a follow-up question to which you may make another response using one of the permitted 'response tracks' (see 4 above). On no account must you use more than six words in an answer and you must avoid telling the truth at all costs.

6 Steps 4 and 5 are repeated for as long as possible. Points are scored as follows:
– if you never answer the original question you get 10 points;
– if your parent gets to the truthful answer, they get 10 points.

7 You score bonus points for making changes in your parent's appearance or manner as follows:
– parent's voice rises in pitch: 5 points;
– parent's voice rises in volume: 5 points;
– parent's face goes red: 10 points;
– parent's veins stand out on neck: 20 points.

8 Your parent scores bonus points as follows, by making you:
– blush: 5 points;
– tell the truth: 5 points;
– slam a door: 10 points;
– threaten to leave home: 20 points.

9 If, at any point your parent stops asking questions, then you have won the game.

10 If, at any point you run out of answers (or run out of the room) your parent has won the game.

In the tense silence that typically follows a game of **KILLER PING-PONG** *you may find it helpful to read a chapter or two from this book — especially if you lost!*

CONTENTS

A dog's life
(When it's hard to agree)

My brain slowly managed to focus as I lifted my head from the pillow. I'm not a morning person and it always takes a while to get life back into gear after the pleasure of a night's sleep. This was a particularly sleepy morning and my mind hesitantly crawled through the data that it needed to feed into my system before I could get up.

'What day is it?' I enquired of my memory bank. This was always the most important question to suss out first since I'd once mistakenly risen and dressed for school at 7.30 am on a Saturday. I'd been halfway down the street before the total absence of any of my school friends alerted me to my error. Fortunately, no one had seen me or I would never have lived it down, but it was a close thing – too close, so I now always double-check which day it is before getting out of bed.

'Think brain, come on,' I pleaded with my grey matter, and eventually I remembered that yesterday had been church, football and a visit from Brad – a Sunday. 'Oh no, today must be Monday.' There could be no doubt. OK, next question, what time is it?'

I sent my hand on a mission from under the duvet and instructed it to grab my Bart Simpson alarm clock from the chair beside the bed. It returned having accomplished its task and after some negotiation with my Seeing Department I managed to persuade my right eye to open far enough to look at the digital display. '7.15. Oh, stress,' I groaned, 'time to get up.' But despite my efforts to emerge into a recognisable human life form my brain failed me at that critical moment, shutting down all my systems and sending me back to sleep. The next thing that its numbed sensors picked up was the sound of Mum at close range and talking fast.

'Gary, for the last time, will you get up you lazy lummox. It's quarter to eight and time you were on your way. I don't know. What's the point of you having an alarm clock if you never turn it on?' It wasn't really a question, at least not one which demanded an answer but in my confused and dozy state I attempted one nonetheless.

'Well Mum, the trouble is if I do set it I never hear the thing go off – it's just not loud enough. Some days I wake up before it goes off and then I hear it, but if I'm already awake then there's no point in it going off. Of course, what I really need is a louder alarm clock that can wake me up in time to hear this one. Then there would be a point to setting this one, I suppose. But otherwise...'

Mum interrupted. 'Gary, you're rambling and making no sense whatever, as usual. Come on, it's time to get up. Your breakfast is on the table and I need your lunch box so that I can pack your sandwiches. Where is it?' I swung my legs out of bed and came to a sitting position, stretched and yawned loudly before saying, 'I don't know. It's here somewhere; probably in my school bag still I think'. Mum made for the corner of the room where I had thrown my bag when I'd returned from school last Friday

'In your school bag? I wish you'd do what you're told and take it out when you get home from school instead of leaving it in your bag all weekend. It's not hygienic. It should be washed as soon as you get home,' she lectured. By this time she had my school bag in her hand and was about to open it. As I watched her fumble with the straps, vague warning bells sounded at the back of my brain. Unfortunately I couldn't interpret their significance until it was too late and Mum was beginning to search my bag for the missing lunch box.

'Gary, what have you got in here?' she asked. 'This bag weighs a ton.'

Suddenly everything came into very sharp focus indeed and I instinctively attempted a diversion. 'Mum, you can't say that anymore,' I ventured.

'What, exactly, can't I say?' she responded, hesitantly, at least temporarily thrown off course.

'You can't say that things weigh a ton. It dates you terribly Mum. Tons don't exist any more. What you should say, if you must use such an expression at all, is that the bag weighs 1016.05 kilograms. Of course, it doesn't sound the same, I do realise that, but ...'

Mum's icy look froze me into silence. 'Gary, shut it.

8

I know what you're trying to do. The issue here is not how many killer whales there are in a ton...'

'Kilograms, Mum, not "killer whales",' I corrected and then wished I hadn't since it only stoked the fires of her increasing anger.

She continued to delve deeper into my bag as she snapped, 'I don't care whether it's killer grans, kiss-a-grams or kipper flans, what I do care about is why your school bag is full of tins of dog food. Gary what's going on? It may have escaped your notice but we haven't got a dog – or any pet, come to that. Where did this stuff come from? You didn't steal it, did you?'

What a strange question! I dived head first into her rising tide of questions, 'Oh that's right. Think the worst. 'Course I did. Armed with my bike pump and wearing the balaclava that Gran knitted me for Christmas I daringly held up the corner shop, clearing out their entire stock of Pedigree Chum before making a daring escape on my skateboard which I'd left revving outside. Honestly, Mum!'

This response, which I thought to be quite witty, only succeeded in raising the temperature even more. Mum fired back with, 'Don't you try to get clever with me, you sarcastic so-and-so. The fact is you've got a dozen tins of dog food here and we haven't got a dog.'

'No, that's right,' I shouted back. 'We haven't got a dog. And why not? Because you won't let me have one. I've asked time and again and all I get is "no" or "maybe when you're older".'

Mum, not to be shouted down, replied, 'Gary, we've talked about this a thousand times. Despite what you say, I know who'd end up looking after it. Dogs need exercise, you know, and it'd be me that would have to give it, wouldn't it? And it costs a fortune to feed them. Who'd pay for that? Me, again. There's not enough money to feed us both, never mind a pack of wolfhounds.'

I tried to calm everything down as I explained, 'I don't want a pack of wolfhounds, just one would do nicely and I know it'd need exercise and I know it'd cost a lot to feed. That is precisely why my school bag is full of tins of dog food. I thought that if I could prove to you that I really wanted a dog then you might give in and let me have one. So I decided to buy two tins of dog food a week out of my pocket money to prove to you that I would help look after a dog if you let me have one. I kept them at school in my locker, but I was running out of space so I brought them home on Friday to hide them under my bed but I forgot to take them out. There you are, now you know.' I looked at Mum hoping to see some reason to hope in her eyes but all I could see was sheer disbelief.

Her mood was confirmed as she said, 'I don't believe I'm hearing this. You've been buying dog food when we haven't got a dog hoping that I would think that such irresponsible behaviour would earn you a puppy? Well, forget it. You cannot have a dog and if all you can do with your pocket money is waste it on pet food for pets that we don't even have, then you'll find your allowance being stopped quite soon too.'

It wasn't the best start to a week that I've ever experienced. Breakfast was eaten in moody silence, and as I made my sullen way to school I reflected that it was all so unfair. Why do Mum and me have to get into so many verbal games of **KILLER PING-PONG**? She asks a question, I give an answer. She makes an accusation, I get cross, she gets crosser. I raise my voice, she shouts... Back and forward it goes, without getting either of us anywhere – except into bad moods. I wish there was a way of taking the pong out of it all.

Surviving life at home: *when it's hard to agree*

Here are some guidelines on how to handle hassles so that things get sorted out and not left to go from bad to worse. (Incidentally, all relationships occasionally go wrong and some of these guidelines might also help you when you don't see eye to eye with your friends or your teachers.)

Take a look inside

If someone is acting selfishly or unkindly then it's bound to make things worse whatever the rights and wrongs of the issue that is being discussed. Make sure that your attitudes towards your mum (or whoever) are in order. The Bible gives some sound advice:

> Let us therefore stop turning critical eyes on one another. If we must be critical, let us be critical of our own conduct... *Romans 14:13, J B Phillips*

Before loading all of the blame onto your mum, take a look at yourself. Are you treating her with respect as God expects you to? Are you accepting her right to make the final decision in the matter? Are you considering her feelings and trying to look at the issue through her eyes? These are all things that are down to you and if you miss out on your responsibility to have the right attitude to your mum, then you'll be for ever having rows with her. Take a look inside yourself and be ready to change if necessary.

Don't duck out

If things are not sorted out they will not usually get better by themselves. I once had a small rash appear

11

on the back of my hand. I thought it would get better if I just left it, but over the next few weeks it spread and then it itched and then when my skin began to blister I decided I ought to go to the doctor! She took a quick look at it, gave me some cream to rub on and within a couple of weeks everything had returned to normal. If only I'd gone to get it looked at sooner I'd have been saved weeks of itching and discomfort.

In just the same way if something is causing an irritation between you and your mum you must get together and really talk it through and not keep having heated arguments that don't really settle the issue, but just make matters worse. Take the initiative and when you and she are both calm (*not* when you've just been at each other's throats) ask if you can talk it through. Choose a time when you can both be free and then say exactly what it is you want to talk about.

Share your own feelings

When you talk things through with someone who you disagree with there is often the temptation to make out that everything is THEIR fault and to start accusing them of all sorts of things. 'YOU never listen', 'YOU don't care', 'YOU'RE not interested in what I want' are all the sorts of statements that lead a discussion directly back into a game of *KILLER PING-PONG*!

Rather than criticising the other person, try explaining how YOU feel about the issue under discussion. For example, instead of 'YOU never listen,' try 'I find it hard to know how to tell you how I feel.' Instead of 'YOU'RE not interested in what I want' you could try, 'I feel upset sometimes when you seem too busy to take an interest in what I'm doing'.

Listen

It has often been pointed out that God gave us two ears and one mouth but most of us still manage to do twice as much talking as listening! The Bible advises us to:

> Listen before you answer. If you don't you are being stupid and insulting. *Proverbs 18:13*

Well, you can't get much clearer than that, can you? Sure you've got a point of view too, but if you listen politely and carefully to your mum's, then maybe she'll be more inclined to listen carefully to yours.

> Everyone must be quick to listen, but slow to speak and slow to become angry. *James 1:19*

If you haven't understood the point that your mum is trying to make, then ask her to put it another way until you really are able to see it from her point of view. There's an old American Indian saying, 'You should never criticise the way someone walks until you've tried to walk in their moccasins'! Try to really listen to what your mum is saying and see what it means to her if your stereo is making the walls shake or if you don't get home at a reasonable time at night.

Be creative

As you listen to your mum and she listens to you, try to think of as many different ways as possible of solving the problem. When you discuss things calmly there are often many more possibilities than you first thought. For example, in the story the issue is whether or not Gary can have a dog. It may seem a simple choice – either 'Yes, he can' or 'No, he can't'. Here are a few more options that could arise if Gary

13

discussed the thing with his mum.

a) Gary can't have a dog but he can have a different sort of pet.
b) Gary can have a dog, but not until certain conditions have been met (for example, his mum's income goes up enough to be able to afford to keep it).
c) Gary can't have his own dog yet, but his mum offers to place an ad in the local paper to see if there is an elderly person in the neighbourhood who would like Gary to help exercise his or her dog.
d) Gary can have a dog but only a small one which needs little exercise and is cheap to keep.

Anyway, whatever the problem, there is normally usually more than one answer. So think creatively and be willing to accept less than you initially wanted – compromise is an important part of negotiating. If you find that you really like one idea, but your mum really likes a different one, keep talking and listening until you can agree.

Be patient, stay cool

But what if things still don't go your way? One of the facts of life is that we don't always get our own way in every situation. (It's probably as well we don't, or we'd become totally selfish people.) However, when we don't get our own way or when we only get a part of what we wanted then we can get upset and resentful and those feeling are dangerous with a capital 'D'!

Staying cross with your mum means that you haven't forgiven her. Unforgiveness is a very serious issue. Did you know that the Bible outlaws *KILLER PING-PONG*?

> Get rid of all bitterness ... and anger. No more shouting or insults, no more hateful feelings of any sort. Instead be kind and tender-hearted to one another, and forgive one another, as God has forgiven you through Christ. *Ephesians 4:31,32*

Did you notice those last few words? Forgive 'as God has forgiven you through Christ'. God forgave us 'through Christ' when we didn't deserve it and before we'd even asked to be forgiven. If you feel that your mum has wronged you, then the right way to respond is with forgiveness – whether she asks for it or not.

It can't be much clearer can it? Forgiveness means to carry on with life as though the wrong thing had never been done (whether or not you get the dog!).

Elephants in the bedroom

(When brothers – or sisters – cause grief)

Dad stormed into the room like a typhoon at the height of its destructive powers. 'What on earth is going on in here?' he bellowed. It was more of a threat than a question but, nevertheless, it drew the standard reply, 'Nothing, Dad.'

'What do you mean, "Nothing Dad"? Don't give me that "Nothing Dad" business. Just what's going on? From downstairs it sounded like there was a herd of elephants up here,' he retorted, still full of threat. (Personally, I found the comparison fascinating. How did Dad know what a herd of elephants would sound like if released into Greg's room? Had it ever happened in his experience? If so, when and where – and what was the effect on the floorboards? Who had managed to round up the elephants and how had they got upstairs in the first place? I was interested to find out more, but now did not seem like the time to ask.)

Dad looked around and a brief inspection of the room didn't appear to reveal anything too amiss – certainly no prancing pachyderms (look it up in your dictionary!). There was Greg, ten stone of well-developed fifteen-year-old brother, sitting on his bed looking out of the window and there was me, glasses perched dangerously near the end of my thirteen-year-old nose sitting next to him and inspecting the Leeds United posters on his wall. So far, it all looked perfectly normal and if it wasn't for the muffled whimpering sounds eerily invading the temporary silence of the room we may have got away with it.

'What's that noise … where's it coming from?' asked Dad as he continued to look around the small room inquisitively. It didn't take long before the noises were identified as coming from underneath the mattress on which Greg and I were sat, still all wide-eyed with innocence.

'Whatever… Get off the bed, you two,' commanded Dad. We duly obeyed and as we stood, so the mattress seemed to take on a life of its own. It heaved and rocked until first a hand then an arm, then another arm, a beetroot-coloured face and finally the small frame of Matt, our little brother appeared, struggling valiantly into the daylight.

'I hate you, I hate you, I hate you,' he screamed as he virtually flew across the room and started punching me with all the strength of an eight-year-old Lennox Lewis.

'Matt, stop it. Stop it. STOP ... IT!' Dad repeated himself as Matt's indignation continued to flow out through his fists. Having stopped, Matt's anger-flow slowed and he ran, crying from the room. Dad turned on Greg and me.

'I suppose you think that's funny do you? Proves you're tough does it? Putting an eight-year-old under a mattress and sitting on him is the "in thing" for proving your manhood these days is it?'

'No Dad,' we muttered in unison, eyes fixed on the floor, minds figuring an escape route. There was none.

'Well, would you mind explaining yourselves then?' he asked. As it happened we did mind, but nevertheless Greg spoke up. After all he was the oldest and it was his bedroom. 'Dad he's just such a pain. Matt and me...

'Matt and I,' corrected Dad.

'No, Dad, it was definitely Matt and me – you were downstairs,' countered Greg, apparently genuinely puzzled by Dad's attempt to correct his grammar. I thought it was going to prompt a 'don't-you-be-so-darned-cheeky' lecture from Dad but, fortunately for Greg, Dad let it pass.

'We came in here to play a computer game. Tom's borrowed a new one from a friend at school. We loaded it up but when I picked up the joystick it fell to pieces in my hand.' Greg was going slowly, hoping that Dad would see where the root of the trouble really lay.

'What do you mean "fell to pieces"?' queried Dad.

'Someone had taken all the screws out of it. No prizes for guessing who,' prompted Greg.

Matt, who'd got over his fit and had appeared at the door of the bedroom to listen to the rocket that he expected us to be getting from Dad, suddenly disappeared again. But not suddenly enough!

'Matt. Matt, come here,' ordered Dad. Matt came

here and was confronted by Dad holding a handful of electronic components and black plastic parts that he had gathered from the top of Greg's desk and which, in a previous existence, had been a computer joystick. 'Do you know anything about this?'

It was a needless question. Matt had a well-known addiction to dismantling anything that was held together with screws. When other boys of his age were requesting *PlayStation* games and footballs as gifts for birthdays and Christmas, Matt was asking for power-tools, hammers and pliers. When other peoples' school-bags were full of games kit, reading books and lunch-box, Matt's was crammed with wire-cutters, spanners and screwdrivers 'just in case'. Asking whether Matt knew anything about the removal of the screws from the joystick was about as necessary as asking Michael Schumacher if he knows how to drive!

Matt's face answered the question. 'Guilty,' it said. Dad followed up with a second question before passing sentence. 'Why Matt? If I've told you once, I've told you fifty times – you're not to take apart things that are still useful. You know that, so why did you take the screws out of the joystick?'

'I wanted to see how it works,' sniffed Matt, his trembling lower lip betraying his inner distress. 'And when I took the screws out, I put them in my pocket so that I wouldn't lose them, but then I forgot that they were there and I put my jeans out for washing and when they came back the screws weren't there.'

'Oh, brilliant! So not only have you destroyed the computer joystick, but you've also bunged up the washing machine with screws. If the pump jams and I have to call out someone to fix it, the bill comes out of your pocket money my boy.' Dad had been calming down, but this latest revelation had refuelled the fires of his rage. 'For goodness' sake why can't you just leave things alone? Go to your room, I'll sort you out in a minute.'

When Matt had taken his sobbing departure Dad turned to Greg and me again. 'And as for you two, you ought to know better than to pick on someone half your size – whatever he'd done. You could have really hurt him under that mattress. What if he couldn't breath?'

Then he'd die, I thought, still smarting at being hassled by Dad for something that was really Matt's own fault. If he hadn't taken the screws out of the joystick none of this would have happened. I began to argue my defence, 'I'm sorry Dad, but...'

'But, nothing.' Dad returned. 'You're both on extra chores for the rest of this week, and while you're doing them you can think about how to behave like civilised human beings.'

It didn't seem fair. As always, Matt causes the problems and we get it in the neck. He'll probably get away with a ticking off and maybe the confiscation of an odd screw driver or two, while we get to wash up for every tea time this week. Brothers (or sisters) – who'd have 'em?

Surviving life at home: *when brothers – or sisters – cause grief*

Not all brothers and sisters are doomed to exist in a state of perpetual warfare (honestly), but just in case you ever get any problems with yours here a few bits of advice which should help.

Let them be themselves

It's sometimes surprising how brothers and sisters brought up by the same parents in the same family can be so different from one another. It's quite normal though and the secret of living with 'different' people is to learn to accept their differences.

Maybe you like certain things and your brother (or sister) likes others. Or perhaps he's revoltingly lively in the morning but needs to go to bed early, whereas your body clock is the exact opposite.

Personal differences do not mean that one person is right and the other is wrong, but simply that each of you is different. Learn to laugh at your differences. Enjoy being you and allow your brothers or sisters to enjoy being themselves too.

Make allowances

Brothers and sisters have to live together during some of the most difficult years of their lives because during the time from birth to teens we change in so many ways.

We change PHYSICALLY (our bodies develop), MENTALLY (we can understand more about ourselves and our world) and EMOTIONALLY (our feelings and moods go through lots of changes – especially in teenage years). We don't choose these changes – or even always want them – but we sometimes find that they've happened anyway.

Family life can be made much more pleasant if all the people involved take the time to try to understand the changes that are happening in one another's lives and then make allowances for them.

Be an encourager

We all know how nice it feels when someone bothers to say a simple 'Thank you' or 'Well done' to us. We also know how unpleasant it feels when people criticise us or put us down.

You probably know the old story of the man who was trying to get his stubborn old mule to move. He shouted at it, kicked it and hit it with a stick but all to no avail. It just sat there. He then had a brainwave. He took one of the sticks with which he'd been beating the animal, tied a carrot on a piece of string to one end of it and dangled the carrot in front of the donkey. Immediately the donkey got up and tried to reach for the carrot and as the man continued to hold it just out of reach it kept moving forwards in the very direction that the man's punishment had failed to get it to go. The 'encouragement' of the tasty carrot was far more effective than the bashings and beatings.

Bashing them with a stick or dangling a carrot in front of their nose will probably not help your relationship with your sister or brother – and neither will constant verbal abuse! But a few words of encouragement might! Go on, take the risk. Give it a go. Try dishing out a few comments like 'Well done', 'Thanks', 'That was good' or 'I couldn't do it that well'. Keep it up for a few weeks and you may well be amazed at the difference it makes.

Do not overwind!

That instruction was often printed on the kinds of clock that had to be wound up with a key because if you turned the key too many times you risked overstraining the spring and causing damage to the mechanism inside.

Maybe if we all walked around with a similar warning printed across our foreheads, we'd treat one another rather differently. 'Do not overwind – this human being will suffer serious strain resulting in possible breakdown if too much pressure is applied!'

There is a very simple rule for getting on with brothers and sisters: DO NOT OVERWIND. If you're winding up your brother or sister to the point where they are getting upset or angry you've gone too far, so back off and walk away before the situation gets out of hand.

Respect other people's property

You know what it's like, you take your Walkman on the school trip, you settle into your seat on the coach, stick the headphones on, press 'Play' and ... nothing. SOMEONE has had the nerve to whip the batteries out of YOUR Walkman without so much as a please or thank you. You're furious!

But then, next week, when you can't find your swimming goggles anywhere and you're late already, you just can't resist the temptation to creep into little brother's bedroom and 'borrow' his. Trouble is they're not adjusted for your head and the elastic snaps when you're putting them on. Now he's furious!

Taking what is not yours without permission is

wrong and often causes a lot of stress between brothers and sisters. The Bible gives three simple bits of advice which may help.

a) Be generous
Jesus' teaching on possessions is pretty radical.

> Give to everyone who asks you for something, and when someone takes what is yours, do not ask for it back ... if you lend only to those from whom you hope to get it back, why should you receive a blessing? Even sinners lend to sinners ... No! ... lend and expect nothing back. *Luke 6:30,34,35*

So, if your brother or sister wants to borrow something, don't get in the habit of always saying 'No'. Learn to be generous, even when it isn't deserved because Jesus says that when we do that we are behaving like God himself who 'is good to the ungrateful and the wicked' (Luke 6:35).

b) Be thoughtful

> Do for others just what you want them to do for you. *Luke 6:31*

This piece of advice given by Jesus is sometimes called the Golden Rule of Relationships. If you don't want people taking your stuff without asking, don't take theirs. If you want the things that you lend out returned in one piece, then make sure you return the things that you borrow in one piece.

c) Be forgiving

> ...forgive one another, as God has forgiven you through Christ. *Ephesians 4:32*

24

OK, so all this generosity may be thrown back in your face and a brother or sister may take advantage of your kindness. Your things may not get returned or may get returned broken (with or without an apology!). At times like that it is tempting to make big threats like, 'You're never going to borrow ANY of my things EVER again!'

Statements like that are very understandable, but forgiveness is a really important part of family relationships and forgiveness means giving people a second chance – even when they don't deserve it. It means lending the CD even when the last one was returned scratched. It means loaning the bike even though last time it came back with a puncture. Forgiveness means that what happened last time is no longer relevant to what you're asking for this time.

People who bear grudges are miserable, and they make others miserable too. So, be a forgiver and spare everyone the grumps.

Communicate when cool

The Bible says that there is a 'time for silence' and a 'time for talk' (Ecclesiastes 3:7). Or to put it another way, there's a time to speak up and a time to shut up.

Trying to sort things out when everyone is really upset is a waste of time. No one is thinking straight and no one wants to listen to reasons for what happened, so it's a 'time for silence'.

However, it is important that issues and problems in family life don't just get left unsorted. When everything has died down and people seem to be in a reasonable mood again, go back to them and try to talk the problem through. If you feel that you get picked on because of your little brother's behaviour, go to your dad when he's cooled down and say something like, 'Dad, I'm sorry for that hassle earlier but sometimes I feel upset when I seem to get into trouble for what other people have done. Can we talk about it please?' I'm sure you'll get a better response, because, when he's calm, it's a 'time to talk'.

The first barbecue of summer
(When it's hard to love your parents)

When does summer begin? Some people go by the date, some people look out for swifts and swallows and some people wait for the temperature to hit 28 degrees. In our household there is a sign more certain than any of these that the promise of spring has turned into the reality of high summer – the announcement of the first family barbecue of the year. When Dad dons his apron and appears in the back garden clutching a bag of charcoal in one hand and a box of fire-lighters in the other you know that summer has arrived.

27

Dad is convinced that he is God's gift to outdoor cookery and has consequently nominated himself Master of Ceremonies at all family barbecues. He insists on taking charge of every detail from beginning to end (but strangely 'the end' always stops just short of any washing up that needs doing). Mum, on the other hand, always treats these occasions with a mixture of gratitude at not having to cook and reservation about having to clear up the devastation that inevitably results from Dad's handiwork. One particular occasion comes to mind from last year.

As I returned home from school I was greeted at the gate by Mum who was going out.

'Hello love. Had a good day?' (She always asks me that but never stops to hear the answer just in case it's 'No'). She continued, 'Your father's come home early and suggested that we have a barbecue so I'm just popping down the shop to get a few burgers and buns.'

Yes, and to keep out of Dad's way, I thought as I carried on into the house. Dad was in the kitchen trying to prise apart two frozen sausages with a carving knife. It was not a sight for the faint-hearted!

'Oh, hi, Alex. Bet you didn't expect to see me here. Got away early for once. Thought we'd have a barbecue, so I'm just getting everything ready. The secret of a successful barbecue is in the preparation. Preparation and patience, that's what it takes – preparation and patience.' This was Dad's standard pre-barbecue speech. I'd lost track of the number of times he'd told us that you needed 'preparation and patience for a good barbecue'.

'I'll get changed and give you a hand if you like,' I volunteered, although I knew the answer that I'd get before I'd even offered. He'd say 'No'. He always did. That's the main reason I volunteered!

'Oh, no need. I can manage – but thanks for offering,' he responded, right on cue.

By the time I'd got changed Dad was in the back garden, so I sat on the lawn to watch the Master, whose left hand was now swathed in bandages, set to work. As always it was like a well-run military operation. The barbecue itself was placed to take maximum advantage of today's wind direction and Dad was painstakingly piling individual pieces of charcoal on top of a complex pattern of fire-lighters which he'd arranged in the base of the barbecue. After several minutes' painstaking work, he'd arranged four pyramids of charcoal each sitting on its own fire-lighters.

It was just at that moment that Jamie, my kid brother, returned from school. He threw the back gate open and ran down the path as though he was being chased by a dog. It turned out that there was a very good reason for his behaviour – he WAS being chased by a dog, a very large red setter who belonged to a family that had just moved in down the road. In case you don't know, red setters are famous for their long red hair, their gentleness and for the large streak of lunacy that runs right through them. This one only wanted to play, but Jamie, who knew nothing of the mental instability of these creatures, feared the worst and fled straight indoors slamming the door behind him.

The red setter, deprived of his potential playmate, decided to do a couple of circuits of the garden before returning home and he was on his second lap when, for reasons known only to himself, he tried to hurdle the barbecue. Sadly, his ambition was greater than his athleticism and he rather spectacularly crash-landed in a heap of charcoal and fire-lighters. Dad, who'd been watching this extraordinary performance of canine vandalism with mouth agape, made for the dog in a rush and the startled animal regained his senses in time to clear the garden fence before Dad got at him with the barbecue tongs.

'Stupid thing. People that let their dogs run loose like that ought to be put in a dogs' home,' he thundered.

'Don't you mean the dogs ought to be in a dogs' home?' I asked, thinking that in his anger he'd got his words mixed up.

'You heard what I said,' he grunted, as he got on his knees to retrieve the scattered pieces of charcoal.

A bandaged hand and an upturned barbecue had not got proceedings off to a good start. If Dad was in a good mood he could just about cope with the demands of barbecuing burgers, but woe betide all of us if things went wrong. And things had already gone outstandingly wrong before even one match had been struck!

Eventually the pyramids were rebuilt and Dad gave the coals a good dousing with the 'BBQ Odour-Free Smokeless Lighter Fluid' which had over-wintered in the cupboard under the stairs.

The 'Odour-Free Smokeless' bit was a recent innovation since a barbecue last year when the fumes from the 'Odour-Full and Smoky' fluid that Dad was using at the time had been taken by the wind and blown though an open window into next door's kitchen setting off their smoke alarm and asphyxiating their guinea pig. We don't think that our neighbours, who were out at the time, realised what had caused their smoke alarm to be screaming at their dead guinea pig when they returned, but in the circumstances a change to 'Odour-Free Smokeless' seemed like the best move.

Anyway, the lighter fluid was Dad's insurance against

the fire-lighters not working, and the use of both usually meant the coals were glowing at cooking heat in no time at all. He struck the match. He always prided himself with using just one match, but this time it fizzled out with a disappointing 'spht'. This did nothing to improve his already frayed temper and muttering something about 'showing the charcoal who was boss' he once again gave it a generous dose of the 'Odour-Free and Smokeless'.

Another match, another 'spht'. More lighter fluid, followed by several more matches and 'sphts'! Although the coals were not getting any hotter, I could feel the rising tide of frustration raising Dad's temperature more than somewhat. I decided to remind him of some first principles. 'Preparation and PATIENCE, Dad. That's what it takes to make a perfect barbecue.'

'I can do without your wisecracks thank you very much. I don't know what's wrong with it. It's never been this difficult to light.'

Just then Mum reappeared at the gate carrying a bag of burgers and buns. 'Everything OK? I'm sorry I've taken so long. I expect you're ready for these now.' Her gaze fell on the flame-resistant charcoal and without thinking or stopping to assess Dad's mood she added, 'Oh, you've not even got it alight yet. Are you losing your touch?' She didn't know it, of course, but it was not the most helpful comment that she could have made and sadly for her it set Dad off into one of his moods.

Poor Mum. He almost shouted at her, 'No I have not lost my touch and I don't need you to come swanning in here making sarcastic comments. If you're so blooming clever you can tell me why this wretched thing won't light. And don't tell me to put any more lighter fluid on the thing because I've already drenched it in the stuff,' he added.

Mum looked at the empty bottle of fluid and seemed to be on the verge of speaking. She swallowed a couple of times, then said quietly, 'That's not barbecue fluid.'

'Oh and what is it then? Come on then if you're so clever.' Dad was at his worst when he was like this.

'It's distilled water that I keep in the cupboard under the stairs to use in the steam iron. If you remember we finished that bottle of fluid at the end of last year and I washed it out to use for the water for the iron.'

I thought Dad was going to get violent. 'You stupid woman. Why didn't you take the label off? You mean that thanks to your rank inefficiency I've soaked the barbecue with distilled water?'

No answer came. None was required. Anyway he was still going on. 'Well that's ruined that. I don't know. I come home early for once, I get attacked by carving knives and chased by lunatic dogs and then, as though that weren't enough, this whole venture is sabotaged by my thoughtless wife. I'm going out,' he said as he threw his apron onto the lawn, 'You can fix your own tea.'

Surviving life at home: *when it's hard to love your parents*

Families would be great if it weren't for the people in them, wouldn't they!? The truth is that, whilst some families certainly work better than others, 'ideal' families only exist in fiction. All families have good points AND bad points and each family member has strengths AND weaknesses.

God is very realistic about what he expects of us when other people disappoint us. He doesn't expect us to disown them, nor does he expect us to be able to change them. He simply expects us to keep loving them.

The Bible gives a lengthy definition of love in 1 Corinthians 13. Here is part of it:

> Love is patient and kind; it is not jealous or
> conceited or proud; love is not ill-mannered or
> selfish or irritable; love does not keep a record
> of wrongs; love is not happy with evil, but is
> happy with the truth. Love never gives up; and its
> faith, hope and patience never fail. *1 Corinthians
> 13:4–7*

Love in the Bible – the sort of love that God expects of us – is not to do with how we *feel*, but to do with how we *decide to behave*. Here are FOUR LOVING DECISIONS that you can take, based on the verses from 1 Corinthians.

1 Decide to be patient

'Patience' comes twice in these verses and we're also told that 'love never gives up', so being patient is obviously an important aspect of loving someone. Being patient means giving someone another chance.

It means telling them that you care about them even after they've been moody. It means hoping and praying that one day they'll be able to change.

When your mum or dad are getting all worked up about something, there's probably not a lot you can actually do (and please note — this is not a good moment to start playing a game of *KILLER PING-PONG*!). Sometimes you just have to be patient and wait for them to get a grip on things.

2 Decide to be kind

If we want to love someone we must decide that, no matter how they behave towards us, we will continue to be kind to them and not allow ourselves to retaliate. Bad behaviour can be catching so watch yourself!

The loving way is Jesus' way — continuing to be kind, even when under pressure. Do you know the story in Matthew's gospel about the armed soldiers arresting Jesus in the garden at Gethsemane? Jesus' friend, Peter, was armed with a sword, and when he saw that Jesus was about to be taken away, he lashed out and cut off the ear of the High Priest's slave, Malchus (a case of 'ear' today, gone tomorrow?!).

Anyway, Jesus saw what the hot-headed Peter had done, and rather than joining the fight he picked up the ear, caught up with Malchus (who must have been hopping all over the garden in pain!), and miraculously repaired his head by sticking his lopped lobe back in place.

Peter fought wrong with wrong, but Jesus gave us the example of combating wrong with kindness — I'm glad that Christians follow Jesus not Peter, aren't you?!

3 Decide to be faithful

To be faithful to someone means to be loyal to them and not to let them down – to stand by them through thick and thin. That's quite easy when the person concerned is being nice to us, but when they aren't, it's a bit harder!

Let's get an illustration from Jesus again. After Jesus' arrest he was taken to be interrogated and the methods used were pretty brutal. As Jesus looked up from being beaten and spat at, his eyes met the eyes of his friend Peter, who was close by, watching what was happening.

Peter was scared that if people knew that he was a friend of Jesus then he would be beaten up in the same way that Jesus had been. So when people accused him of being Jesus' friend, Peter bottled out and denied that he even knew him. Now it was at this point that Jesus showed his loyalty and faithfulness to Peter. It would only have taken one word of greeting from Jesus to identify Peter as his friend and get Peter arrested too. But Jesus didn't call out, 'Hi, Pete'. He just looked at Peter and then looked away again. Even while Peter was betraying Jesus, Jesus refused to betray Peter. He showed his love for Peter by being faithful and loyal.

There may be times when you get tempted to tell a lot of other people just what your mum or dad are like at home. Of course, you wouldn't be lying, but it might mean not being faithful or loyal to your parents and probably wouldn't help the situation much either.

Now, if things are really tight at home, try to find one or two trusted friends who can support you and pray with you – and who can then keep their mouths shut about it!

4 Decide to forget

Love does not keep a record of wrongs. Do you? When someone is trying to change the way they behave one of the worst things that can happen is for old mistakes to be constantly raked up and thrown in their face.

A few days after Peter's failure to stand up and be counted as a friend of Jesus, he'd gone back to his fishing business in Galilee. It was early in the morning and from his fishing boat Peter could just about make out a familiar figure standing on the beach. He strained his eyes and recognised that it was Jesus himself standing there! Too impatient to wait for the boat to be rowed to shore, Peter dived into the water and swam to see Jesus.

As we read about the incident in John chapter 21, it's very interesting to notice, not only what Jesus said to Peter, but also what he didn't say!

Remember, Peter had let Jesus down by publicly denying that he knew him but Jesus doesn't drag all that out into the open, perhaps because he knew that it would crush Peter to have all his faults pointed out to him.

In just the same way, it's quite possible that your mum or dad already feels bad enough when they know they've lost their cool at home. If you keep on about it, it's just going to make them feel worse and more stressed and then, in turn, even more likely to get in a mood!

So, love your parents, even (perhaps, especially) when you don't feel like it. Decide to be patient, to act kindly, to be loyal and to tear up that record of wrongs. This is no fix-it-quick remedy but in the end, it's the course of action most likely to help a tricky situation improve.

How to avoid Nether Wallop
(When there's not much money)

'Where are we going on holiday this year then Dad?' It was an innocent question and I wasn't really prepared for the uneasy look that it brought to Dad's face.

'Er, holiday. Don't know. Haven't given it much thought really.' A pause, then, 'Look Stacey, the truth is that I doubt we'll be able to afford much of a holiday this year. Money's a bit tight and there's bills that have to be paid before we can think much about holidays. Maybe things will pick up a bit later in the year, but I shouldn't hold out any great hopes.'

'What do you mean, Dad? No holiday at all?' I was deeply disappointed. We'd never been rich enough to go abroad but we'd always at least managed a week away in a caravan at Yarmouth.

'Well, you could always go and stay at Nether Wallop with your gran. She always likes to see you.'

Oh thanks, Dad, thanks so very much. I could just imagine the conversations at school.

'Hey guess what, we're going surfing in Australia for our holiday this year.'

'Wow, mega! We're going white-water rafting in Borneo. How about you, Stacey?'

'Oh I'm being treated to an all-expenses-paid week in Nether Wallop.'

Have you ever been to Nether Wallop? Probably not. It's noticeably lacking in even the most basic requirements for a decent holiday. No beach, no swimming pool, no amusement arcades, no hot-dog stands. No people (well, none under sixty-five anyway), no theme park, no Pizza Hut – in fact no shops of any description. It would be far quicker to say what Nether Wallop has got, than to list its shortcomings. It has got twelve, mainly thatched, cottages, and er ... that's about it really.

'Dad, you cannot be serious. Not a week in Nether Wallop!' I protested.

'Well, you could go for a fortnight if a week's not enough,' returned Dad, somewhat missing the point I felt.

'No, Dad, what I meant was that a holiday in Nether Wallop is a contradiction in terms. Holidays are all about fun and excitement. Nether Wallop offers about as much fun and excitement as a bucket of cold custard.' I was impressed by my own argument. Dad wasn't.

'There's no need to get all "iffy". We can only do what we can do. If the money was there, we'd all be off to the South of France like a shot, but as you know, it's not.' His tone told me that the matter was closed, as far as he was concerned.

It always came down to money – or rather the lack of it. Lack of money was why I had to wear my sister's second-hand school uniform, and why, when the rest of the class went to France on the exchange trip I stayed in school helping Mr Bateman paint scenery for the school play. Lack of money is why I keep very quiet when my friends are all on about their latest CDs and why I always find an excuse when they ask me to go to see a film with them. Lack of money was about to land me in Nether Wallop, unless I negotiated the next few minutes very carefully.

'Dad are you serious about letting me go to Gran's?' I enquired, deliberately softening my tone of voice.

Dad looked up from his *Evening Post*. '*Letting* you go?' he queried. 'You sound like you actually want to go. A minute ago you were sounding off about Nether Wallop like it was a terminal disease.'

'Yes but that was before...' I hesitated just long enough to sow the required seed of doubt in Dad's mind.

'Before what? What's going on in that scheming head of yours?' He was working up a head of steam now and I knew just how to keep him on the boil. One word should do it.

'Nothing,' I answered vaguely.

It worked like a treat. 'Oh yes there is. I've known you for too long to know that when you say "nothing" is going on, there's a strong likelihood that "everything" is going on. Now come on, what has suddenly changed Nether Wallop into Britain's number one tourist attraction?' He was really going for it in a big way now. His paper was lying on the table, forgotten, a mark of his concern at this new turn of events. I knew that a few more well-chosen words would do the trick.

I spoke hesitantly, as though I didn't really want to give the information. 'It's just that … last time I was there … I made … a new friend. That's all. It'll be nice to meet up again.'

'New friend? What new friend? I don't remember anything about a new friend.'

'No, well I never mentioned' – (here goes, hit him with THE key word) 'him.'

'HIM is it? Boy, then?' he asked, somewhat unnecessarily, but it proved that I had him well and truly on my hook. If there is one thing that Dad is more worried about than his lack of money, it's me getting involved with some boy that he doesn't know (and he's not too keen on me getting involved with most boys that he does know for that matter!).

'Yes. Terry, his name is. I met him last time I went to Gran's on my own – you know when you were away on that training course.' Time to reel in the fish, I think. 'He's twenty-one and he's got the most powerful motorbike I've ever seen.'

That did it. 'TWENTY-ONE! MOTORBIKE!! Do you seriously think that I'm going to let you go off on holiday with a twenty-one-year-old biker? You're off your head my girl. I'd sooner take out a bank loan and take us all white-water rafting in Borneo than see you spend a week in Nether Wallop with this Terry and his band of bikers. What do you take me for? You think you can just do what you want and that I'll take no notice. Well let me remind you that I make the decisions in this house.'

Well, most of the time Dad, I thought.

Surviving life at home: *when there's not much money*

Is money an issue for you? Do you get as much pocket money as your friends? How about money for the essentials of life — you know, mobile phone, CDs, computer games, and at least one cinema trip a week? Here are a few ideas that might help you come to terms with your financial situation, and handle what money you have got wisely.

Some things are more important than money

Love for example! It's not unusual to read in the papers about people who have had everything that money could buy, but still feel unhappy because they had no one who loved them.

If you get on well with your parents (well, most of the time) that's brilliant. There are loads of kids at your school who would willingly live without some of the things they have if only they felt that their parents loved them.

Maybe you'd like your parents to be able to give you more 'things' than they can at present — and maybe *they'd* like to be able to give you more. But if they are giving you their love, then they are giving you the best thing that they have.

Don't believe the adverts

Adverts are not designed to tell you the truth about the world or yourself. They are only designed to get you to spend your money. You know how it works...

The girl in the advert sprays herself with the latest perfume — 'Tunnell' from Channel. Wearing the Channel 'Tunnell' she wafts down the staircase in her office smiling contentedly (she's happier).

Men look up from their desks and nod approvingly as she floats past them (she's become a better person).

Finally, as she enters her boss's office he distractedly breaks off his phone conversation and gawps in wonder at this apparition that's just entered (she's become more popular).

And all because the lady wears Channel 'Tunnell'!

Now what happens? Thousands of girls rush out to buy Channel 'Tunnell'. But when THEY wear it, they don't become happier or more popular. No, the only reaction is, 'Cor, what the bloomin' heck's that niff. Someone trod in something?'

Maybe some of your school friends are taken in by the power of advertising but there's no need for you to be. True happiness is not found by having enough money to buy every new product that comes onto the market.

Be grateful for what you have got

If you compare yourself to your well-off friends all the time then you'll feel more and more unhappy. But how about taking a look at some of the people in your school who are worse off than you?

Or, how about looking even further to other parts of the world where people of your age have nothing except maybe the few rags that they stand up in. They've never owned a toy, or slept in a house and many times they've gone without food for days on end. Maybe they've even lost their parents to war or disease. It's a painful thought isn't it, but it's reality for millions in our world today, and when we measure our lifestyle against theirs we suddenly realise just how rich we really are.

Be generous with what you've got

One of the traps that we can fall into when we haven't got much is that we try to protect it so as not to lose it. When it's taken us a year to save up for our CD player we're going to be far more protective of it than someone who had theirs given to them and who knows that should they lose it, they'll just be given another one!

Now, at one level, it's clearly a good thing to take good care of your possessions. It would just be wasteful to treat everything as though it were disposable. But there is a very short step from being careful with what we have, to being selfish.

Jesus taught us that we all belong to one another and that we must put other people first. Jesus taught whole-hearted, open-handed generosity. 'People not things' could have been his motto.

Jesus' first followers took his radical attitude to possessions so seriously that the Bible says about the early church in Jerusalem:

> No one said that any of his belongings was his
> own, but they all shared with one another
> everything they had. *Acts 4:32*

Now that's generosity!

Even if you still feel you've not got much, share what you have and make God chuffed!

Think of your parents

If you are finding it difficult to cope with what you have, then I'm sure that it's doubly difficult for your parents. They may not show it to you, but they may well feel terrible about not being able to give you all that they'd like to.

If that is the case, it would be really helpful to them if you could try to be realistic about what you expect them to be able to provide. Sure, you might want a DVD player for your birthday, but is it fair to put that pressure on your parents? You know they can't afford it, yet they may well feel that they are letting you down by not being able to provide what you want. So why not ask for things in their price-range — they'll feel pleased to be able to get you what you want and you'll at least be fairly sure that you'll get what you ask for.

A party popper in the sermon
(When you're not sure about church any more)

A game of **KILLER PING-PONG** was in full flow. Points were being scored on both sides with Dad just nudging ahead on the score-board.

'It was only a party-popper for goodness' sake!'

'Yes, but why did you let it off in the middle of the sermon?'

'I've told you hundreds of times. I didn't mean to let it off. I was bored and I found the thing in my pocket and as I was fiddling with the string it just went off...'

'Why did you take it to church in the first place? What was it doing in your pocket?'

'It must have been left over from last night's party, I suppose.'

The inquisition went on and on. Dad was in a real strop and there was no hiding place from his fury. How had it happened? My mind drifted back over the evening's events as Dad's disapproving lecture droned on.

It had all started in time-honoured fashion. We'd arrived at church at about 6.15 in time for the 6.30 service. Mr Hewitt was on 'Welcoming' duty and greeted us with hymn books, plastic smile and an eye-wateringly firm handshake. Mum and Dad always sat at the back – right hand side, third and fourth seats in – and as they took their places I went to sit with some of my friends nearer the front.

By 6.25 all the regulars were in their places. Mrs Peters was installed, fully armed with cough sweets which she would unwrap noisily during the opening prayer (no one had ever heard her cough, but everyone had heard her cough sweets). Miss Milligan, an elderly and partially deaf spinster, had taken her usual seat just in front of us (row three, second seat in) and adjusted her hearing aid to take in the pre-service performance of Mr Morgan at the organ.

Everyone was in place as at 6.29 (and forty-five seconds) Mr Grimethorpe the minister emerged from the vestry and strode to the front of the church, whilst the short stream of attendant deacons who followed him from the vestry filtered to their places amongst the congregation.

6.30 precisely and we were off on the well-known path of hymns, prayers, collection, notices and Bible readings (one from the Old and one from the New Testament) all topped off with one of Mr Grimethorpe's sermons. The pattern was so predictable that my friends and I had devised a number of mental exercises that could be employed to deaden the dullness of it all. Here's a sample of our 'Lower Loxley

Evangelical Church Service Survival Guide'.

1 Count the hairs on the neck of the person sitting in front of you and divide by the number of verses in the first hymn.

2 See how many words you can make out of Grimethorpe.

3 Guess in which of tonight's hymns Mr Morgan will miscalculate and start playing a verse that isn't in the hymn book.

4 Guess how many cough sweets Mrs Peters will unwrap during the service.

5 Pretend that you are a robber and work out the best way of stealing the collection plate without being noticed.

6 Add up all the numbers on the hymn board and divide by the number of legs in church (chair legs, table legs, people legs could all be counted).

7 Look through the hymn book to find the hymn writer with the most outrageous name (James Augustus Toplady takes some beating!).

8 Guess how many times Miss Milligan would adjust her hearing aid during the service.

9 Work out how many seconds there are between the present time and the end of the service (tricky one this, since by the time you've finished the calculation the 'present time' has changed, so you have to start again).

10 Work out what would happen if someone accidentally filled the glass from which Mr Grimethorpe sipped during his sermon with vodka rather than water.

This particular evening I'd worked my way through all ten points of our survival guide and it was still only 7.15. A full quarter of an hour of sermon left and nothing to do but listen to Mr G in full flow, all about 'the timeless wisdom of God as manifested in the genealogies of Matthew chapter 1'. The only thing that was timeless as far as I was concerned was this service and in desperation I rummaged in my pocket for something to enliven the last fifteen minutes of the ritual.

Usually all that my pocket contains is empty sweet packets, a bus pass and a foreign coin or two, so imagine my delight when my hand closed on a small plastic bottle-shaped object – a party-popper, left over from Fiona's birthday party last night. Keeping the popper concealed in my hand, I carefully brought it out of my pocket and began twiddling the string round my finger. Here was a new diversion for our list: 'How many times can you twist a party-popper string around your little finger?' I'd managed to twist it three times around when disaster struck. With an explosion, the wretched thing just went off in my hand sending small ribbons of tissue paper in all directions! The effect on the service was dramatic.

Miss Milligan, whose hearing aid was turned right up so as not to miss a single word from Mr Grimethorpe, leaped a clear twenty centimetres into the air and screamed as though she'd been shot.

Mr Morgan leapt to his feet to see what had happened, and got his foot stuck in the organ pedals, filling the church with a booming low-pitched growl.

Mrs Peters swallowed her cough sweet whole and actually started coughing – indeed choking – for the first time in living memory.

My friends, festooned with party popper streamers, literally shook with silent delight at my misfortune and all the while Mr Grimethorpe, who'd turned a sort of yellowish-grey colour, like the true professional that he is, kept right on preaching with barely a pause for breath (although what with the organ booming and Mrs Peters choking no one could hear a word that he was saying!).

The remainder of the service has been erased from my memory-banks but here I was now, two hours after the event, still getting a right old ear-wigging from Dad. It wasn't fair. I didn't want to go to church in the first place. I only go because Dad and Mum would throw a fit if I said I wanted to go to another church (or worse still to no church at all).

I awoke from my reverie to hear Dad saying, '...and if you ever do anything like that again your mother and I will leave you at home on a Sunday evening.'

Mmm, now there's an offer that ought to be looked into. Anyone got any left-over party poppers?

Surviving life at home: *when you're not sure about church any more*

It's not unusual for young people who have gone to church with Mum or Dad as children, to get to the point where they have to work out for themselves why they are there!

The 'inside' story

Imagine a football match where all the stands are packed with people who are totally uninterested in watching football. You can imagine that the amount of support that they would actually give to the teams on the pitch would be pretty small. If those same people were forced to go week after week, some of them would end up wondering, 'Why am I here?' and finding things to do to fill the ninety minutes of boredom whilst the match is in progress. The problem isn't with the sport of football or the individual players on the pitch, but with the attitude of the 'supporters'.

In a similar way church services are occasions when God's 'supporters' can get together to praise and worship him and spend time learning about him – but if the people in the 'crowd' aren't too interested in him then the whole thing will seem empty, pointless and boring. On the other hand if people turn up at church with a real desire to thank him for all that he has done in the past week and hoping to learn something new about him – then those people are likely to get something out of the service, no matter what happens in it.

Why DO you go to church? Do you go to praise God and learn about following Jesus, or not?

No second-hand faith

YOU CANNOT GO ON LIVING ON YOUR PARENTS' FAITH. As a teenager, you are now at the stage where you must think about the whole thing for yourself and decide where YOU stand.

The first question that you should address is: 'Do I want to be a follower of Jesus Christ or not?' When you've got to grips with that, THEN, you can think about which church will be best for you to attend. All young people who are brought up in Christian families and taken to church by their parents have to get to this point of personal decision. It's no longer a question of whether to please Mum or Dad, but a question of whether YOU will be a follower of Jesus or not.

Joshua was a great leader of Israel. He led them into the land that God had promised would be their home after their years as slaves in Egypt. After many battles, most of the land was won back for them to settle down in. At the end of his life Joshua assembled all of the people and issued them with this challenge.

> Now then ... honour the Lord and serve him
> sincerely and faithfully. Get rid of the gods which
> your ancestors used to worship in ... Egypt and
> serve only the Lord. If you are not willing to
> serve him, decide today whom you will serve.
> Joshua 24:14,15

Joshua's words could have been written down just for you! If you are not willing to serve God, then you must decide who you will follow. You have a choice.

Church will ultimately only 'make sense' to people who have made a decision to put God first in their lives. People who have little interest in following Jesus

– or people who are sitting on the fence – will be turned off by church.

Choosing a 'good' church

Having challenged you to consider where you are with God at the moment, let's look at the issue of choosing a suitable church to worship him with. Some people enjoy the church they were brought up in and stay there until they leave home. Others find that a clean break with the church where they've grown up can give a chance to work out their own faith without being constantly referred to as someone else's son or daughter!

If you do decide that a move would help you here are eight pointers to guide you:

1 Look for a church where Jesus is talked about a lot.
2 Look for a church where the Bible is used a lot.
3 Look for a church where prayer is taken seriously.
4 Look for a church where they are trying to reach non-Christians.
5 Look for a church where the people really seem to care for one another.
6 Look for a church where there are some other people of your age.
7 Look for a church that is as close as possible to where you live.
8 Look for a church where you can be involved and use the gifts and skills that God has given to you.

DON'T COMPROMISE ON THE FIRST FIVE POINTS! There's not much hope for a church where Jesus is ignored, the Bible remains closed, prayer is a low priority and the inward-looking members don't like each other! Be honest about your own church. If it scores highly on the above rating system then don't leave it without a lot of thought and prayer – churches like that can be hard to find!

However, if you do decide a change is necessary, and you manage to find a good church to attend, I'm (fairly) sure that your parents won't mind. Break it to them gently. Explain why you want to make a fresh start and the good points about the church that you're wanting to go to, without appearing to rubbish the church that you've been brought up in.

Finally though, remember that there is no point changing church if you're not turned on to God inside. It won't make any difference – it's possible to be bored in any church if you don't go there with the right attitude.

The Archangel Bill

(When you're parents aren't Christians)

He'd been there every day for the past week, sitting cross-legged on the pavement outside Woolworths. The hand-written card on the ground said it all, 'I'm Bill. Hungry and homeless. Please help.'

Surprisingly, and despite his obvious need, he looked raggedly cheerful as he played a selection of Christmas carols on his mouth organ. Each time someone dropped a coin in his upturned hat, apparently without missing a single note of the carol that he was playing, he uttered a polite 'God bless you, friend.' There was something about him that I just couldn't get out of my mind and as the week went on I thought about him more and more.

How could I help him? After all it was Christmas, the season of good will, love and peace to all mankind. Bill was a 'mankind' – of sorts – and so surely he deserved to enjoy Christmas just as much as the rest of us.

I wasn't sure what to do so I prayed about it that night and asked God to show me how to help Bill. I didn't get any particularly clear answers but in my Bible reading there was a verse that said, 'Remember to welcome strangers in your homes. There were some who did that and welcomed angels without knowing it' (Hebrews 13:2).

I read and reread the verse and slowly light began to dawn. So that was it. That's how he managed to stay cheerful despite his awful circumstances. That's how he managed to talk and play the mouth organ at the same time. The answer was suddenly clear. Bill was an angel in disguise. Cool. A real, live undercover angel outside Woolworths.

Now what should I do? I'd never come across a plain-clothes angel before. I read the Bible verse one more time looking for inspiration and there it was, as plain as a spot on your nose. I saw what must be done. 'Welcome strangers into your homes,' it said. So I decided that I had no alternative but to invite Bill home for Christmas.

I'd only made my amazing discovery about Bill's true identity just in time. The next day was Christmas Eve, so it was with a real sense of mission that I got up the next morning and after a hasty breakfast made my way to the shopping centre to meet my angel. As I walked, I rehearsed what I would say. I wasn't too sure how you addressed angels so I practised a number of alternatives.

'Excuse me, O Winged Wonder...' No, that sounded stupid. How about 'Glorious Creature of Light, I wondered if you'd like to come back to my place for a bit of nosh.' Mmm, that was getting closer, but still not quite there.

After pondering a few more alternatives, I settled for a plain 'Hi there, Your Angelship, I'd be dead chuffed if you'd come home with me for a meal and a change of clothes.'

I turned the corner by W H Smith and I could hear the wheezy strains of Bill's harmonica growing louder as I drew nearer to where he was sitting. As he paused to wipe his lips between carols, I summoned up my courage, went up to him and delivered my invitation.

'Hi there, Your Angelship, I'd be chuffed dead if

you'd come home with me for a change and a meal of clothes.'

My nerves had got the better of me but he looked at me, smiled and said, 'Well now, there's an offer. And what would your parents think of a tatty old fellow like myself turning up unannounced on Christmas Eve?'

Good point! In all my excitement about discovering Bill's true identity I'd not stopped to think about how Dad and Mum would react. On reflection, I didn't imagine that they'd be too impressed to be honest, but then again God had told me to help the Archangel Bill and it WAS Christmas. Even though my parents weren't Christians, surely they wouldn't begrudge one of God's own messengers a mince pie and a glass of sherry (even Father Christmas used to get that much on Christmas Eve, and Bill was a real live cherub!).

Hastily weighing up Bill's question, I blurted out, 'Oh, they won't mind a bit, they'd be pleased to see you. We often have strangers in our home at Christmas.' (That was nearly true. We often had Aunt Mildred and they don't come much stranger than her!)

Bill asked again, 'Are you sure they won't mind?' I'd never realised just how cautious off-duty angels were.

'Yes, no problem. Come on, it's not far.'

A few more moments of reassurance and Bill was shuffling alongside me, homeward bound.

It was only as we walked up the front path that feelings of doubt began to eat at my good intentions, feelings which intensified as we entered the front door and Mum's voice rang out from the kitchen, 'Is that you Tony? You weren't out long. Did you forget something?'

'Hi, Mum. Could you come out here a minute? I've got a surprise for you,' I called, a false seasonal cheerfulness covering my anxiety. Never a truer word was spoken, for as Mum emerged from the kitchen, she caught sight of her first ever angel and, yes, she did seem to get a surprise. Shock might have been a better word for it, because she stood rooted to the spot, mouth frozen in the open position, staring at Bill in what I took to be a most awestruck manner. So complete was her paralysis that it was left to Bill to break the ice.

'Hello, Missus. It was very nice of you to invite me home for Christmas. Proper cold it was out there on that street.' He looked around. 'Nice place you got. Reckon I'll be quite comfy here.'

Mum's mouth thawed enough for her to gasp, 'Tony. Can I have a quick word with you in the kitchen? Now, please.'

With the kitchen door pushed to, leaving just enough of a gap for her to keep an eye on our guest, Mum went on the attack, hissing between closed teeth,

'What in the name of Father Christmas are you playing at? Who is that man and why is he standing in our house? And what's all this about being comfy for Christmas? Answers please, and fast.'

I began to explain about good will and Christian love. About how God had let me know that Bill was an angel in disguise and how the best way to help lost cherubs was to invite them in to your home. I even offered to get my Bible and read her the actual verses, but the look in her eyes told me to shelve that plan for the time being! It was useless trying to explain. If only she was a Christian perhaps she'd have understood, but as it was she seemed completely closed to seeing Bill as anything but a homeless old scrounger.

We went out to where Bill was still standing. To Mum's credit, her voice was calm and disarmingly sweet as she began, 'Look, er… Bill is it? I'm sorry, but there's been a terrible mistake. Tony had no right to invite you back like this. We couldn't possibly take you in over Christmas – we just haven't got the room.'

Bill's face showed no sign of disappointment as he said, 'Oh, I see. Well don't worry Missus, I thought your lad was probably a bit out of order when he invited me but nothing ventured, nothing gained, eh? No hard feelings.'

He raised a hand to open the front door but something in his manner had caught Mum off-guard. To my surprise and, as she claimed later, against her better judgement, before she knew what she was saying she'd offered Bill a cup of coffee, a mince pie and one of Dad's old overcoats which had been put out to be taken to the Oxfam shop!

So maybe it wasn't so bad in the end. The angel was fed and clothed, Aunt Mildred duly arrived (wearing a Chicago Bears American football helmet for some reason) to occupy the spare room unaware that a celestial being had been evicted to make room for her and I'd done my best to do what God wanted done.

It's tough, though, being the only Christian in the house and this isn't the first time that I've had differences of opinion with Mum and Dad over my faith. Maybe I should try to get a bit of advice on how to handle things before God sends another angel my way.

Surviving life at home: *when your parents aren't Christians*

Living as a Christian in a home with parents that don't share your faith can cause conflict at times. There are almost bound to be differences of opinion, and when there are the important thing is that you react in line with your Christianity. Here are a few guidelines to help:

Put your own house in order

Paul (the one in the Bible), writing to Christian young people puts it this way:

> Children, it is your Christian duty to obey your parents, for this is the right thing to do. *Ephesians 6:1*

God has made your parents responsible for your life until you are at an age when you must take that responsibility for yourself. Now God's not dumb – he fully understands the tension that's created if your parents are not Christians and you are. He knows that at times you want to do what he wants but that maybe your parents don't always agree.

If being obedient to your parents results in you being unable to do what you believe God wants, don't worry. God is happy at the moment with your good intentions, knowing that one day you will be old enough to put those good intentions into practice without your parents stopping you.

Katy was a teenager who wanted to be baptised. Her non-Christian parents thought being baptised was a way-over-the-top-religious-thing and said 'No way'. What should she do? She felt like her parents were keeping her from obeying God?

In the end Katy decided that the best course was for her to tell God that she wanted to be baptised, but that for the time being she was going to obey him by obeying her parents.

She then told her parents what she had decided. She wasn't prepared for what happened next. Her parents were so pleased that she was putting their wishes first that they changed their minds, and allowed her to be baptised after all!

Not every conflict has such a happy ending but Katy's story does illustrate that with a bit of creative thinking it can be possible to satisfy your responsibility towards God and towards your parents!

Do 'em good

Peter (Jesus' friend not the piper who picked a peck of pickled peppers) wrote this:

> For the sake of the Lord submit to every human authority ... for God wants you to silence the ignorant talk of foolish people by the good things you do. 1 Peter 2:13-15

No one is suggesting that non-Christian parents are ignorant and foolish – but there is an important principle here. You see, if your love for Jesus makes you a real pain at home then your parents will not only moan at YOU, they will probably think pretty badly of God, Jesus, Christians and everything to do with church as well.

Peter's advice is that you silence your parents' criticism of all things Christian by showing them the good side of Christianity – 'the good things you do'.

Take Jesus' example of serving others and become

a servant in your own home. Wash up without being asked, make your bed (more than once a month), offer to wash the car (without charging!). In short, be an example of practical, serving Christian love to your parents. It'll probably blow their minds. They might try to get you to see a doctor! But whatever, it will certainly prove to them that your faith isn't just a selfish thing that makes you awkward to live with, but something that makes you a better son or daughter than they'd ever thought possible.

Enlist prayer power

Jesus said this:

> Love your enemies and pray for those who
> persecute you... *Matthew 5:44*

Hopefully you don't see your parents as your enemies, but maybe at times you might feel a bit picked on for what you believe. If you do, then how do you respond? Throw a paddy? Lock yourself in the bathroom? Maybe. But how does Jesus tell us to respond? By loving and praying for those who are giving us hassle.

Here are four things that you could pray for:

1 Pray that God will show you ways of being the best daughter or son that you can be for your parents.
2 Pray that you have the inner strength to obey your parents and love them – even when they appear to be acting unreasonably.
3 Pray that they'll start thinking seriously about God because of what you see in you.
4 When they've hurt or upset you, pray for forgiveness for anything you might have said in the

heat of the moment which maybe caused them to feel hurt.

These are all prayers that God wants to answer, so when you pray, really believe that God is hearing and that he will answer!

Get some advice

It's often hard when you're right in the middle of all the aggro at home to think things out clearly for yourself, so it's worth finding someone a bit older and wiser — and obviously someone who is able to see things from a Christian point of view — to chat it all through with.

If only we had more aerosols
(When parents always seem to say 'NO!')

Mum was in concerned-parent mode. 'Now look Kathryn, you're sure you'll be all right? It's just tonight and we'll be back by 10 o'clock in the morning. I've left a contact number…'

'…by the phone, Mum, I know; you've told me enough times!'

Once a year Dad's boss organises an outing for everyone in the company to go up to London to watch a show and stay overnight in a hotel. This year, for the first time, Mum had asked if I'd sooner stay home on my own when they go, rather than stay with Aunt Nancy as I'd done in previous years. Although I always enjoyed staying with Aunt Nancy, I had decided that being left with the house to myself had certain advantages, so I'd agreed to give it a go and stay home alone.

Today was the day and the nearer we got to the time for their departure, the more stressed-out Mum was getting. She was speaking again, 'There's plenty of food in the fridge. I bought a few extra bits in case you get peckish.'

I'd already been shown the 'few extra bits' and I couldn't resist saying, 'Mum, do you really think that I'll get through half a cold chicken, a tub of coleslaw, four yoghurts, six penguins, a pound of cheese, a tin of tuna chunks, half a cucumber, a whole lettuce, two litres of Coke and a bag of oven chips between four o'clock this afternoon and ten o'clock tomorrow morning? It does seem a little over-the-top just for one person for one evening don't you think?'

Mum was not to be deterred. 'Well, I couldn't bear to think of you starving while we were enjoying ourselves,' she countered.

I was about to ask in which circumstances she *could* bear to think of me starving, but she was off again. 'Don't forget. Keep the door locked at all times, put the cat out at 6 o'clock and don't stay up all night watching the TV.'

This was getting monotonous so I interrupted, 'Really Mum, it's no big deal. You've written all this down and you've said it about a million times. What next, a video version? I'll be OK. Now just you and Dad go off and enjoy yourselves and leave me to pig out.'

It's true that staying in the house alone didn't worry me but I also had other reasons for wanting Dad and Mum to get off out of the way. They didn't know it, but I'd invited a few friends round for the evening and the sooner they went, the sooner I could ring round and say that the coast was clear. Dishonest, maybe, but too good an opportunity to miss and anyway if I asked their permission they'd only say 'No'. 'No' is their favourite word, in fact they like it so much that they use it all the time, for example:

Me: 'Can I stay out late tonight to...?'
Them: 'No.'
Me: 'Can I borrow five quid to...?'
Them: 'No.'
Me: 'Can I go to Jane's house to watch...?'
Them: 'No.'

Me: 'Can I miss youth group on Friday to...?'
Them: 'No.'

(Come to think of it there really ought to be a new rule
for **KILLER PING-PONG** that heavily penalises parents
for using the word 'No' more than once in a game. It
really mucks up the game when they are so
monosyllabic!)

I could go on, but you get the drift I'm sure. It
doesn't matter what the question or reasoning behind
it is, anything I say in which they even smell a question
mark gets the big N.O. so I'd decided not to ask about
having my friends round but to just go ahead and
organise it. It won't do any damage and anyway, what
Mum and Dad don't know about they can't worry
about – so it's kinder to them too!

Eventually Mum and Dad were on their way and a
few quick phone calls summoned my friends.

Tracy was the first to arrive, followed soon after by
Sam, Helen, Angela and Wendy who'd walked round
together. The oven chips were just beginning to brown
when the doorbell rang. It was Mandy, who
unexpectedly had brought her new boyfriend Kevin.
This was a worrying development and one that I
received with mixed emotions. If anything should go
wrong and Mum and Dad discover my little plan then
the absence of males in the house would have been one
of my lines of defence. Kevin's arrival had therefore
removed one of the planks of the arguments that I'd
been preparing in my head 'just in case'.

Anyway, I didn't have the guts to turn him away, so
in he came. He seemed decent enough, despite his
Arsenal T-shirt.

Having eaten cold chicken and semi-frozen chips,
penguins and coke, we all settled down to watch the

video that Angela had brought with her. It was a thriller called *Dye Hard* and was about a mad scientist who'd invented an indelible colourant which he threatened to release into the water supply of Los Angeles unless he was paid a trillion dollars by the city authorities.

The film had just started when I remembered that the cat was still in, so I left the room to put him out in the garden. It took longer than expected because he had crept into my wardrobe and I couldn't find him, so about five minutes had passed when I returned to pick up the threads of the film. As I made my way back to the sitting room I was beginning to feel quite relaxed. The evening was going well. Kevin had proved no real problem and Mum and Dad would be well on their way to London by now. Great. Back to *Dye Hard*.

As I pushed open the sitting room door I just could not believe what greeted me. The room was filled with a pall of smoke and the smell of burning tobacco hung heavily all around. A quick glance around revealed the culprit. Kevin had lit up a cigarette. He turned as I entered and, all innocence, said 'Hi, Kat. Don't mind if I smoke do you? The others thought you would but I was sure you wouldn't.' The 'others' — my so-called 'friends' — continued to stare at the TV screen in an attempt to distance themselves from Kevin and his decision to light up.

Calm and reasonable I was not. I almost screamed, 'Put it out you pin-head. I don't care if you want to kill yourself' (in fact at that stage I would willingly have helped him to do it!), 'but my parents will kill ME if they come home and find the house full of cigarette smoke. I don't believe you could do this to me, you stupid, selfish, thoughtless...' I ran out of adjectives to describe Kevin, but he had got the message and sheepishly extinguished the offending article. Too late

– the damage was done.

Despite watching the rest of *Dye Hard* with the windows wide open, at the end of the evening curtains, carpets, clothing and even the cat who had crept back in through the open windows, all stank of smoke. As everyone left I wondered what I was going to tell my parents but, still suffering from mild shock at Kevin's sheer thoughtlessness, I could think of no good reason to explain away the lingering stink.

After a poor night's sleep I virtually ran to the sitting room to sniff the air. It was no good, the smoky aroma still filled the room. What was I to do? Calm down, Kathryn. Think logically. The smell of smoke wouldn't go, so maybe the answer was to fill the house with so many other smells that the smell of smoke was disguised. Brainwave or what? I couldn't get rid of the pong, but maybe I could cover it up. It was worth a try.

I set about the task with vigour. I left toast to burn under the grill while I gathered every single aerosol that I could find in the house. Fly-killer, deodorant, hair spray and breath freshener — amongst many others — were all squirted in generous quantities over furniture, fixtures and fittings in every room. The combination of smells created some very interesting effects and by the time I'd finished, the house smelt like a cross between a rose garden, a pine forest, a dentist's surgery and a public toilet. Surely not even Mum's nostrils could discern the smell of smoke underneath all this other stuff.

Mum and Dad returned early. I heard the car pull up at 9.40 and the key turned in the front door at 9.42 precisely. I was in my room as I heard Mum enter the front door. She started to call,

'Kathryn, we're home. Where are...' A slight pause, then, 'Good grief, what on earth has happened? What IS that smell? Kat, where are you? Are you OK?'

I appeared at the top of the stairs and met Mum on her way up. 'Kat, what have you been doing? It smells like you've been using every aerosol in the house.' How typical of Mum to be able to analyse things so accurately and quickly, but at least she hadn't noticed the smell of...

'And whoever has been smoking? Kathryn, what HAS been going on here?'

I'll spare you the gruesome details but I expect you can imagine them anyway. Think of the worst strop your parents have ever got into and times it by ten and you'll be near the truth. If only I'd ASKED to have my friends round. If only Kevin didn't exist. If only we had more aerosols! Too late to worry now, but maybe I'll check it out before they go away and leave me on my own again.

Surviving life at home: *when parents always seem to say 'NO!'*

What a mess. And it all started with Kat being afraid her parents would say 'No' if she asked to have her friends round. Thinking about it, parents DO seem to have an unhealthy attraction to the word 'no', particularly when talking to their own children! Let's look at why that is and how you can come to terms with it.

'No' is *a positive word!*

Have you ever thought about why your parents say 'No' so much? Strange as it may sound, it could be because they want what is best for you. They may say 'No' so often just because they love you so much!

According to the Bible, 'Love always protects' (1 Corinthians 13:7, *New International Version*). The fact that your parents love you means that they also want to protect you – and that is often why they say 'No' to so many things that you want to do.

When you were small you were probably into all sorts of things and if parents didn't say 'No' when you were about to use the neighbour's Rottweiler as a trampoline they wouldn't be being very loving (to you or the Rottweiler!).

Even now you are older, your parents will still want to protect you from physical, emotional, mental or spiritual harm. If they think that what you are asking for is going to hurt you, they are more than likely going to give it a straight 'No'.

So 'No' can be a negative answer given for very positive reasons by very loving parents. Far from being a negative word, it can be a word which tells you that your parents love you enough to want to protect you.

Negotiate your independence

You might be willing to accept that *sometimes* your parents are right to say 'No' because what you are asking for is really a bit unreasonable. But at other times they just do not seem to realise that you have grown up a bit since the last time they said 'No' and that now you are capable of being allowed to do a bit more.

Your parents clearly cannot protect you for ever and if you asked them I expect they'd say that they wouldn't want to! But parents are not always very good at taking their hands off and allowing their children to make more decisions for themselves.

It can't happen all at once. When you were first born your parents had to make absolutely every decision for you and as you've grown they have made less and less. One day you will be completely left to make up your own mind about everything, but in the meantime you are somewhere in the middle of that process.

Why not try to talk to your parents about where you are on this journey towards independence? Don't try to talk it through when you are angry with each other or when they've just said 'No' to something! You could ask them for more freedom to make your own decisions in particular areas but be realistic and don't try to get everything you might want at once.

Earn your independence

When your parents see you behaving responsibly and making wise decisions about where you go, when you go there and who you go with, they will probably be more inclined to stop saying 'No' to so many things. Their job as parents is to teach you how to manage your own life properly and in the end it all comes down to trust. The more that they feel able to trust you, the more relaxed they will be about leaving you to make your own decisions. On the other hand if you abuse the trust that they put in you (for example by having friends round when they are away or by sneaking in to see an 18-rated film!), then they may well try to control your life even more. Trust takes quite a time to earn but can be quickly lost. So be patient and be careful not to blow it all by one thoughtless decision!

Are you receiving me?
(When communications break down)

OK, so kicking doors and throwing books about the place might not be the right way to deal with things, but at least it got rid of some of my frustration and anger and it was better than kicking Mum and throwing my little brother about the place! I didn't want to come home like this, in fact I didn't come home like this – it was my welcome home that made me like this.

For most of the day at school things had gone unexpectedly well. It had been the kind of day that I always imagine happening to other people but never to me. In the first lesson we'd got our maths tests back and I'd got 17 out of 20. This was the first time I'd got a mark in the teens and it had prompted a break-time celebration in which cans of coke were shaken and sprayed over all my friends who retaliated in similar fashion with theirs. The celebration had reached its peak when Miss Thorpe entered and caught a jet of celebratory Fanta right between the eyes.

'Whatever … Who did that? What's going on in here? Whatever are you doing? Look at this mess,' she spluttered incoherent and uncomprehending of the great celebration that she'd stumbled into.

'Oh, sorry Miss,' muttered an embarrassed Damon Clark whose Fanta had christened Miss Thorpe. 'But it's a great day, Miss. One the like of which the world has never seen.'

'And I sincerely hope for your sakes that it'll never see such a day again,' she replied, clearly not entering into the spirit of celebration which the occasion demanded. She continued, 'What makes this such a great day that everyone and everything has to get sprayed with carbonated liquid?'

Teachers talk like that. You and me would call them 'fizzy drinks' but teachers have to speak in a kind of code which proves that they've been to university and so 'fizzy drinks' become 'carbonated liquid'.

Different subjects have their own version of this code. For example, in science what any normal person would call a 'rotten stink', your average science teacher calls a 'noxious gas'. In maths a 'squashed box' in every day English becomes a 'trapezoid' in every day maths teacher-speak, and in English a 'naff book' becomes a 'linguistically challenging piece of literary art'.

I ask you! It's no wonder we never learn much when our teachers speak a different language most of the time. (Before I leave the subject I should perhaps warn you that this sort of thing is highly contagious. Last week Mrs Brawn, our school cook, had written 'Tarte a la Berger Anglais' on the menu board but when we actually sampled this 'foreign' delicacy, it bore a disappointing likeness to what in previous weeks had been called shepherd's pie!)

Anyway, back to Miss Thorpe and the great maths test celebration. All things considered she was pretty decent about it. She sent us to Dot the caretaker for some cleaning cloths and made us spend the rest of break washing down the desks that had got accidentally sprayed. Under the circumstances we'd got off lightly and rather than feel fed-up at losing break I felt relieved that things hadn't been worse. (If it had been Mr Flint who'd found us we'd have been cleaning the whole school during every break for the rest of term!)

Next lesson was music. Last week Mrs Blare, our music teacher, had warned us that she was going to be away this week but that she was going to leave some work for us to do. Mr Harmworthy arrived to sit with us, carrying a large pile of marking which he obviously wanted to tackle whilst we did the set work.

As we entered the room we noticed that someone had been in the room during break and left several derogatory comments about Mrs Blare chalked in large letters all over the set work on the board. 'Mrs Blare has manky hair' and 'Mrs Blare's a silly mayor' (I think they meant 'mare') and other comments all in similar vein. It was nothing too rude but once Mr Harmworthy had seen it, it clearly had to go. He immediately set to work with the board rubber vigorously erasing the insulting graffiti without apparently realising that he was also deleting the instructions which Mrs Blare had left for the lesson.

By the time he did realise what he'd done, it was too late and the only thing for it was for Mr Harmworthy to allow us to do some 'private study' for the lesson. That was great because it meant that I could do some revision for the science test scheduled for after lunch and finish the maths homework that we'd just been set, thus leaving myself with a free evening.

Lunchtime was OK – hot-dogs, chips and doughnuts (very nutritious), followed by an impromptu game of five-a-side football (Man United v 10S). All in all then, it was with an unusual feeling of well-being that I entered room H5 ready for the science test.

Mr Davies gave out the question sheets and we all began, in silence of course, to work our way through the test. It was all about the human body. Most of the questions were quite straightforward and what I didn't know I worked out. For example there was a question about bones.

Where in the body would you find:
(a) the cranium?
(b) the sternum?
(c) the fibula?

Mmm, tricky. Well, 'cranium' sounds like it might be like the word 'crane' and your arms are sort of your body's cranes – so I guessed that the cranium is an arm bone.

'Sternum'? Well, the stern is the back of a boat so I suppose the sternum is your backbone.

Now then, 'fibula'. This was more tricky to work out, but a 'fib' was what Mum called a lie and was therefore something you said. Perhaps the 'fibula' was therefore your tongue bone. Well, it was worth a try. At the end of the forty-five minutes I thought I'd probably done quite well and handed in my paper with confidence.

The last lesson of the day was football and just to top the day off nicely I managed to score the winning goal in the game. Admittedly it was an own-goal and gave the victory to the other team but it was a very spectacular own-goal. Mr Purdy our PE teacher said it was the best he'd ever seen! The other members of my team weren't so impressed, but you can't please everybody all the time, can you?

Now that you know how well my day went you will not be surprised that when I arrived home I was itching to tell someone all about it. Mum was the first 'someone' I encountered in the house and before she could say anything I was off.

'Mum, you'll be pleased to know that I had a brilliant

day today.' Mum put down her book and looked slightly taken aback at this most uncustomary of greetings.

Ignoring her air of disbelief I continued all of a rush, stringing the events of the day into one breathless sentence.

'I got a really good mark in maths Miss Thorpe let us off spraying her with Fanta Mr Harmworthy wiped out Mrs Blare so I haven't got any homework lunch was ace the science test was a doddle and Mr Purdy said I scored the best goal he's ever seen.'

I paused to draw breath and awaited the tumult of praise that I thought I'd earned by my day's endeavours but Mum's response hardly came up to expectations.

'Slow down. I didn't understand a word of that. What are you in such a state about? And look at the state of your shoes. How do you manage to get them covered in that much mud? I've told you I don't know how many times to take your old trainers to change into if you must play football at break. And what's that

BUT MUM! I GOT A GREAT MARK IN MATHS!

all down your shirt? It looks like Coke! That'll never come out. How DID you manage to get coke all over you? If you had to do the washing in this house you'd be a sight more careful.'

There was more but I stopped listening. A feeling of intense frustration and injustice welled up within me. I'd done my best. I'd worked hard. I'd got my best ever maths mark and for once, just for once, almost enjoyed a day at school and all I got was this hassle over a few spots of mud on my shoes and a bit of spilt Coke.

'Forget it Mum, just forget it,' I shouted as I ran to my bedroom and vented my feelings by kicking the door shut and throwing a pile of books across the floor. I don't know why I bother trying to talk to her anyway. Maybe I'll just keep my mouth shut from now on. That would be preferable to being ignored or shouted down. How DO you get through to parents?

Surviving life at home: *when communication breaks down*

Everyone knows that feeling of opening your mouth and putting your foot in it, or of saying something in all innocence which gets totally misunderstood. Communication needs working at, so here are Ten Commandments (well, ten suggestions, anyway) for improving your speaking and listening skills.

1 Thou shalt be honest

Sometimes it's easier to say 'I don't care' than to admit that we do care and explain why. For example, if Mum's going out for the evening and you'd hoped to spend some time with her she might say, 'I'm going out tonight, you don't mind do you?'

Now it may be because of the disappointment that you feel inside that you hear yourself saying, 'No, that's fine. I don't care,' when really it's not fine and you do care!

Pretence doesn't help a relationship develop to maturity, so learn to be honest about your feelings.

2 Thou shalt choose your moment

You don't always feel like answering loads of questions and in just the same way your parents have moments when they have got time and energy to chat and times when they've got other things on their minds.

If you've got some weighty issue to discuss the best time is when your Mum or Dad can concentrate on what you've got to say. If necessary, make a booking, tell them that you'd like to chat something through with them and ask them when they will be free enough to talk. Make a time and date and make sure you keep it free!

3 Thou shalt know yourself!

Another aspect of choosing the right moment is to take a quick spot-check on your own feelings before opening your mouth. If you are really feeling up-tight or angry about something it may be better to wait until you've calmed down a bit before trying to talk it through.

4 Thou shalt think first, speak later

There is a good way and a bad way to say almost anything. When you're sharing personal concerns and feelings it's important to choose your words carefully. Here are two different ways of saying the same thing. Which do you think will be more likely to be well received?

a) 'Mum, you're always going out and doing what you want. You just don't care about us stuck at home on our own.'
b) 'Mum, I feel lonely when you're out in the evenings. I'd enjoy spending a bit more time with you sometimes.'

The first statement is said in anger. It accuses Mum and probably makes her feel guilty. The second statement is more a request for help and will probably make Mum feel wanted.

It's worth taking time to plan ahead and find the best way to say what you want said.

5 *Thou shalt learn to share your feelings*

Communication happens at all sorts of different levels from simple statements of fact ('We had pottery today'), through a more detailed look at life ('We had pottery today and my pot didn't work too well') to the ability to share personal feelings at a deeper level, ('We had pottery today and my pot didn't work too well. I really felt upset when everyone laughed at it').

If communication always happens at the shallow level of making simple statements of fact then all those other deeper feelings just get bottled up – and that's not good for us.

Try to train yourself to be open with your parents. Trust them with your *feelings* not just bald facts. It'll sometimes be hard but in the end it will create a far better relationship with them so it is worth the effort.

6 *Thou shalt check that you are being understood*

Despite all your best efforts your parents might still misunderstand what you are saying. How do you know if you're being understood? Simple. Ask! Just say something like, 'Mum (or Dad) I'm not sure I'm putting this very well. What do you think I'm trying to say?'

It may sound like a dumb question but at least it'll make sure that you are really communicating and not getting crossed wires!

7 *Thou shalt learn to listen*

Communication is a two-way thing and all the people involved should feel able to ask questions or put their point of view. When you talk to your parents don't be so full of your own point of view that they don't get a look in.

Ask them for their opinions and really listen to what they have to say. Give them space and let them ramble on a bit if necessary. They'll probably get to the point eventually!

8 Thou shalt guard your tongue

The book of James in the Bible leaves us in no doubt what damage the tongue can do.

> The tongue is ... a world of wrong, occupying its place in our bodies and spreading evil through our whole being ... no one has ever been able to tame the tongue. It is evil and uncontrollable, full of deadly poison. *James 3:6-8*

Wow! Strong stuff, but maybe a good reminder of just what damage our words can do when we speak thoughtlessly or unkindly.

9 Thou shalt – if necessary – 'write' your wrongs

Despite all our best intentions we can still bottle out of opening our mouth. The right moment never seems to come, or else it comes and we miss it!

Well, try writing it all down. Sometimes a letter can succeed where a conversation fails. The advantages of a letter are:

a) You can say exactly what you feel without being put off by other people's interruptions.
b) You can think carefully about what you want to say and have several goes at getting it right.
c) You can leave it with the person to read at a time that is most convenient for them.

d) They can read it several times and think carefully about their response before coming back to you.

OK, so writing a letter to your own parents IS a last resort but it can be helpful and can be a way around those times when something needs to be said but everyone is too scared to say it!

A letter or card is especially nice if you want to say something POSITIVE to your parents (communication isn't only about problems and hassles!). A card saying 'Thanks for being there' or 'Nice pizza, Mum' would probably mean more to your parents than you could ever imagine.

10 Thou shalt be big enough to try again!

You may follow all nine commandments, add in a few of your own and still it may all go horribly wrong.

Maybe your parents don't listen. Maybe they've upset you. Maybe they refuse to let you do something you really want to do. Even if all that – and more – is true, don't give up on trying to communicate with them. Give it another chance – and if it goes wrong again, then give it another another chance!

Sick of being thick

(When parents put you down)

Why did it feel like there was a time-bomb just waiting to go off in my school bag? Why did I walk home more slowly than usual tonight? I suppose it could have something to do with the fact that I was the unwilling delivery service of my very own end of term school report. Expecting you to carry your own school report home was like asking someone to carry the axe to their own execution – sick. But there it was, that was what I was doing.

I not only walked slowly, but also took the long way home. Even so, I only delayed the inevitable by ten minutes or so.

'Hi, Mum,' I called cheerily to the front room where Mum was watching TV. 'I've got my school report here,' I muttered under my breath hoping that she wouldn't hear.

'Is that you, Shelly?' The enquiry came absent-mindedly as the video of last night's *Coronation Street* clearly took priority over my homecoming.

'No, it's Madonna. Just called in to see if you had any odd jobs needed doing, you know washing, ironing, that sort of thing. I'm at a bit of a loose end at present.' The sarcasm was wasted.

'Don't be silly, Shelly. When I said, "Is that you, Shelly?" I obviously didn't mean "Is that you, Shelly?" Who else would come home at five to four in the afternoon? I simply meant "Is that you Shelly?" – you know.'

Precisely! Ah well, at least this little diversion meant that she'd not noticed my muttered announcement about the report.

'Got a school report, did you say? Let's have a look at it then.' Foiled again. Dad says that if she'd been around in the Second World War they'd have used Mum's hearing instead of radar to detect incoming bombers. He may be right.

Still hoping to delay the inevitable I called, 'Yes, I'll leave it on the kitchen table. You can have a look at it later.'

'No, wait there. I'm just coming.' Mum's arrival was accompanied by the distant sounds of the *Coronation Street* theme music wafting in from the front room. The video had ended. If only I'd been home ten

minutes earlier it'd still have been going strong and I could have made my escape. Fate can be very cruel. Mum picked up the brown envelope containing my report with a hopeful, 'Now, let's see what we've got here.'

The next few seconds seemed like several hours. Mum's scrutiny of my report was punctuated by the occasional, 'Oh, Shelly' and 'Really, love'. Eventually this verbal version of the Chinese water torture came to an end and Mum looked at me with the mixture of pity, anxiety and frustration that she usually gave to our dog when he'd been sick on the carpet.

I could bear it no longer. 'Well. How did I do? Don't just stand there looking at me like that. Speak.'

My anxious enquiry pitched me into one of the tensest games of **KILLER PING-PONG** that I had played. Unfortunately Mum had obviously been in training and I was hopelessly unfit.

Mum almost groaned, 'I don't know where to start.' She scanned the report again. Choosing a comment apparently at random, she read, '"Shelly's insistence on using a foreign language in class is most disruptive".'

'Mum, what am I supposed to do in French? We all have to speak in French, all the time. Even Mr James does. What's he on about?' It seemed unfair, grossly unfair. I was about to continue to argue my case when Mum added, 'That comment was written by your maths teacher, Shelly.'

'Oh.' Well it was a stupid subject and as far as I was concerned maths WAS a foreign language. So I'd decided to make the point by speaking in Manganese (a language that I'd made up especially for the occasion).

Mum was reading again. '"Since Shelly broke her glasses she has struggled to see the board or read from her books and is consequently well behind with her classwork this term".' Mum looked at me, perplexed. 'But Shelly, you don't wear glasses. You've never worn glasses. What is Miss...' she referred to the report, 'Miss Hardiman talking about. Has she got the wrong pupil?'

If only she had. Pretending that you had lost or broken glasses that you had never even owned was the oldest labour-saving trick in the book. Surely Mum knew how pointless humanities was. I mean, what is the point in learning how the ancient Incas milked their llamas? I suppose that if one day you were out for an afternoon stroll in the High Andes (happens all the time) you might be likely to come across an ancient Inca-person desperately struggling to survive for the lack of the skill. You could step right in and say, 'Hey there, Mr Inca, don't you even know how to milk your own llama? Goodness me, even I know that, thanks to my humanities teacher Miss Hardiman. Who ever did you have for humanities? I bet you had Mr Ford, didn't you. He only teaches useless things like ...'

'Shelly, are you listening? I'm talking to you.' Mum's rising anger cut across my daydream. 'What does this mean? There had better be a pretty good explanation, my girl.'

That was it. Bad sign. When Mum called me her 'girl' I knew that I was in for it. She continued, 'From Mr Taylor, your art teacher: "Shelly's insistence on wearing a diving mask and snorkel in class has seriously impaired her ability to create anything of note this term." A SNORKEL? In art? Shelly, what's going on?'

'Mum it stinks in that art room. It's right next to the kitchens and you get this awful whiff of boiling cabbage and frying fish. I was just making a point that's all. It can't be healthy to have to sit in that environment...'

'No, and it's not going to be very healthy in your environment here when I've finished with you. I'm really disappointed. You're a lazy good-for-nothing. You're even thicker than your brother – and that takes some doing. Why do you do it? You know you'll only get yourself in trouble. You've always been difficult, right from birth, but this just about tops the lot. Don't know why we ever bothered to have you – course we didn't mean to, but that's another story. Your sister always did so well. Why couldn't you be more like her?'

On and on and on and on. I gave up on this particular game of **KILLER PING-PONG** long before Mum did. It's a stupid game anyway.

Go on Mum, tell me again, in case I didn't catch it last time or the time before or the time before that. Thick am I? Stupid? Unwanted? Careless? I know, I know, I've heard it all before.

Surviving life at home: *when parents put you down*

Being bombarded by negative words hurts — even if we pretend it doesn't, so here are a few thoughts to help you deal with the pain.

Everyone is special

Did you realise that you are the best thing that God ever thought of? Well, OK, not just you but you and all human beings. It's right there in Genesis chapter 1. As each new bit of the world came into being, God stepped back and was 'pleased with what he saw' (Genesis 1:4).

Finally God made human beings, and when he stepped back and looked at the world now, he wasn't simply 'pleased', he was 'VERY pleased' (Genesis 1:31).

Humans were (and are) simply the best part of the world and YOU are one of those humans of whom God thinks so highly. From the moment that you were conceived, God was thrilled at the prospect of another human being coming into his world. Take a look at these verses from Psalm 139:

You created every part of me;
  you put me together in my mother's womb...
When my bones were being formed,
  carefully put together in my mother's womb,
when I was growing there in secret,
  you knew that I was there —
  you saw me before I was born. *Psalm 139:13–16*

There you go. Not an accident, but a special person put together by God himself! When you were born he was delighted and he still is today. No matter what you've done since birth, or what other people have done to you or said to you, God is still totally sold out on you.

No such thing as a useless life

Some of the people in the Bible had the most difficult upbringings imaginable, but God was still able to give them a place in his plans. Moses, for example, was born as a refugee in a foreign country and nearly killed as a baby by the king (Pharaoh). As a young man, he murdered someone and had to run away to the country of Midian to escape execution. What a mess! Refugee, abandoned, unsure of his own identity, a murderer. If ever a man should have had a chip on his shoulder, perhaps it should have been Moses.

But this was the very same man whom God chose to play the major part in Israel's dramatic escape from Egypt. The same man who God directed to perform miracles in the desert and who was thought fit to receive the Ten Commandments from God.

If God could turn Moses' life around, despite what others thought of him or what he thought of himself, he can do the same for you. There is no life that God cannot use – he is the ultimate recycler of lives that other people have thrown in the dustbin.

Words are dangerous

Do you know the old saying, 'Sticks and stones can break my bones but words can never hurt me'? It's a load of old tosh, isn't it. Everyone knows that words DO hurt us, sometimes very deeply.

The Bible's a bit more realistic. Here's what Proverbs 12:18 says:

> Thoughtless words can wound as deeply as any sword...

And the damage is even greater when the words come from people who we love and who we want to love us – people like parents for example!

When other people's words hurt us we can react in a number of different ways.

Live up to it

We can start living up to (or down to!) their expectations. So if we're called 'thick' enough times, we'll start not trying too hard at school – almost as though we want to prove them right!

Retreat

We can try and back away from the people who are hurting us – shutting ourselves away in our bedrooms, spending long hours round at friends' houses or just ignoring our parents, even when we are with them, tortoise-like, retreating into our protective shell.

Retaliate

When we get hurt enough we may feel that the only option we've got left is to fight back. There are several ways that people do this (none of them helpful!). Some people try to hurt their parents by being rude to or about them, others deliberately fail at school because they know that their parents will be upset. In extreme cases, when young people have been really hurt, they might even try to damage themselves – maybe by refusing to eat normally – just to get their own back on their parents.

You see how powerful words can be, and how much damage they can cause. They are like little sparks that light a great bonfire of hurt and resentment, which, once it's ablaze inside us, can get out of control, damaging not only ourselves but others around us too.

This is all a bit depressing! So what can be done? Well, negative words are at their most dangerous when we start believing them. As long as we can ignore them or laugh them off it's not so bad. We need an antidote – something that helps us deflect the lies. We need a healthy diet of TRUTH to take away the bad taste of the lies.

Eat truth

The best medicine that I know of for someone that has been hurt by lies, is to eat a regular diet of truth! Others might say 'You're a waste of space,' but God's truth about you is that 'You're wanted, loved and valued.' Whose opinion do you want to feed on?

You might find it helpful to write out God's perspective on your life on *Post-it* notes. You could carry one in your school bag and sneak a look if things get tough at school or stick one up in your bedroom so that at the beginning and end of the day, whatever people have said you can remind yourself of the truth.

You could start by copying some of these Bible bits out from Isaiah chapter 43.

Do not be afraid – I will save you.
   I have called you by name – you are mine…
   …you are precious to me …
   …I love you and give you honour.
Do not be afraid – I am with you. *Isaiah 43:1,4,5*

(These words were first written to Israel but are true for anyone who loves God.)

Finally, just one bit of practical advice. Try to find at least one good friend who you can trust and who doesn't join in when other people begin to put you down. If there is even one person in your life who is saying something positive to you and about you then you'll find it much easier to swallow these 'truth tablets'!

Healed people don't need bandages

People who are made to feel failures often try to compensate by becoming 'successful' in other ways. They might muck about at school, so that people will pay them a bit of attention or be deliberately unhelpful at home so that they can hurt the parents who are hurting them.

Behaving stupidly or even unkindly can be just an act that people put on to try to cover up their hurts. The trouble is that, if they are not careful, the stupidity becomes a habit and they can't stop even when they want to.

If you can see yourself heading in that direction, stop and think for a minute. If you let other people's hurt change you into an unpleasant person then they've won, haven't they?

I know it seems risky to you if you've been hurt by 'being yourself', but it's a risk that you'll have to face one day. You can't go all through your life trying to be someone else in order to cover up your hurts. Be yourself and you'll probably find that people will start accepting you far more than when you're being someone else!

Vinny and the Duke of Wellington

(When you need to understand what a family is)

Incredible. Unheard of! The whole family gathered together in one place at one time. Great uncles, stepsisters and fairy godmothers – the whole lot were here and they were all here to celebrate my fourteenth birthday. We would never have all fitted in our house so Mum had booked the skittles hall in the local community centre. As I looked around the assembled relatives I realised just what a wide cross-section of humanity was represented in our family.

For starters there was Mum ridiculously overdressed, her size 16 figure clasped firmly but awkwardly by a size 12, bright orange evening dress. It tapered to the ankles so much that each step she took only carried her forward about ten centimetres (the short walk from the car to the hall had taken her thirty-five minutes). Her ginger hair was tied into bunches with green ribbons and she wore long dangling earrings in a shade of green which nearly matched the ribbons in her hair – nearly but not quite. The total effect of the outfit gave her the appearance of an overgrown carrot that was just beginning to learn to walk. Not what she intended, I'm sure.

At the moment she was having a conversation with Grandad who had arrived dressed as the Duke of Wellington, apparently under the misapprehension that this was a fancy dress 'do'.

'Never mind, Dad,' I heard Mum say, 'It suits you very well. Very becoming.'

'Always wanted to be in the army myself, of course,' Grandad replied. 'Volunteered for the Guards during the last war, you know, but they wouldn't have me. Too short, they said. Too short, I ask you!'

Grandad had often reminisced about the war and had often reflected on his rejection by the Grenadier Guards – a rebuff which still hurt him so deeply that every retelling of the story was as full of passion as the time when it was first told in the mid-1940s.

'So I said to that toffee-nosed recruiting officer, "What do you mean too short? Too short for what?" Quick as a flash he said, "Too short for the Grenadier Guards, my good man," stuck-up, la-di-da twit. Well, I wasn't having any of that from a bloke like him so ...'

'You hit him,' interrupted Mum. Grandad could talk for a whole evening about his military experiences and he'd never been further than that army recruiting office in William Street. He could make that story about being turned down last for hours – goodness knows how long he'd have rambled on if he'd been accepted and actually fought in the war!

Seated across the table from Grandad and trying not to get drawn into the conversation about his wartime experiences was my cousin Vinny. He was sixteen years old and profoundly in love with my stepsister Julie who, although aware of Vinny's affections was totally unmoved by them. Vinny had tracked down Julie at her seat next to Grandad and had attached himself to her. In the past his attempts at friendship had been seriously rejected by an uninterested Julie but, never one to give up, Vinny had invested in a book called *How To Impress Someone You Really Fancy* which he had found in a second-hand bookshop. The tone of the book was set by the blurb, which was printed on its back cover. It read:

> In love? Want to impress? Then this book is for you. Award-winning Polish author Dr I Luvzyu explains how to dress to impress, how to smell to compel, how to act to attract and how to natter to flatter the girl of your dreams. If you follow the straightforward advice contained in this one slim volume, you need never again know the embarrassment of rejection by that special someone in your life. Here are some comments from readers of previous editions of *How To Impress Someone You Really Fancy*.
>
> 'I'd never had a girlfriend but after reading Dr I Luvzyu's book I have had fourteen serious relationships and five offers of marriage.' *Martyn, age 18*
>
> 'I used to think there was something wrong with me but since reading *How To Impress Someone You Really Fancy* I've managed to speak to lots of girls – one of whom actually spoke back!' *Donny, age 16*
>
> Look out for Dr Luvzyu's next blockbusting, award-winning encyclopedia of human relationships, *How To Distress Someone You Really Hate* – coming soon to a bookshop near you.

Having read the blurb, you might think that Vinny would have been alerted to the book's potential shortcomings, but no. He'd got stuck right in and had faithfully acted on its every recommendation. So here he was at my party dressed in a tacky imitation-leather jacket, smelling like a perfume factory and staring intently into Julie's eyes as he quoted a poem ('guaranteed to melt the hardest heart') from Dr Luvzyu's book.

Light of my morning, joy of my heart
From by my side may you never depart.
I have admired you for many a week
And your affection decided to seek.

Mere words can't express just how I care
As I gaze on your face and complexion so fair.
A person like you in life comes just once
So I wondered if you'd like to meet me for lunch.

O please do not spurn me or answer me nay
Or else I'll go mad and they'll put me away.
Life without you is like a bike with no wheels
Going nowhere fast – to your heart I appeals.

To be fair to Vinny he did put his heart and soul into it and to be fair to Julie she did try – for a short while at least – not to laugh out loud. But the internal pressure of suppressed humour was eventually too much to contain and she erupted into floods of giggles. As she paused for breath she managed to splutter, 'Vinny what are you on about? Where did you get all that junk? Last year's Valentine's cards? You must want your head examined! What was it again, "Life without you is like a bike with no wheels"?' She collapsed with near terminal mirth once again, before managing to ask, 'Would you do me a favour, Vinny?'

Vinny's face lit up, 'Anything, Julie. What?'

'Get lost,' came the brutal reply, once again uttered through gales of laughter.

Things started to move fast from this point on. Vinny had brought it on himself really but the pain of rejection was so great that instead of getting lost as requested, he picked up the glass containing the remains of his alcohol-free lager and, without hesitation, emptied its contents over Julie's head. This had a dramatic effect on Julie and seemed to be a very effective cure for her previously uncontrollable hilarity. She screamed and sprang to her feet protesting loudly.

Grandad, who'd had a bit too much rum by this point in proceedings – and who had a bit of a soft spot for Julie – immediately sprang to his feet showing surprising agility for a man of his age. The other thing that he showed was the sharp end of the ceremonial sword that he'd hired with his Duke of Wellington outfit. Waving the blade menacingly in Vinny's terrified face he challenged, 'Insult a lady, eh? Young hooligan. Well, we'll see just how much of a man you are. Draw your sword, Sir, draw your sword.'

Meanwhile, Mum, who'd spotted the incident

developing from the high bar stool which she had somehow managed to clamber on to, attempted to hasten to Vinny's aid but misjudged the degree to which her dress rendered her incapable of rapid movement and fell face first from the stool to the floor.

Later, the video which Uncle Roland was shooting all the while made compulsive viewing. Grandad was the star of the show, chasing a white-faced Vinny around the room forcing people of all ages to dive for cover as his increasingly wild sword slashes endangered anyone within a two-metre radius of his sword arm. In the middle of this pandemonium, Mum was left rolling around the room. Cocooned in her orange full-length straightjacket her cries of 'Get me up, will somebody please GET ME UP!' competing in volume with a lager-dripping Julie's screams of 'Vinny, I'll kill you if Grandad doesn't.' It was very colourful.

Of course the whole thing was a disaster. It was certainly a fourteenth birthday to remember, but not one that I'll remember with any affection. I knew it was a mistake getting our family together – I mean some of them hardly know each other, not really family at all – or are they? What makes a 'family' anyway? Just people who live in the same house, or people who are related or what?

Surviving life at home: *when you need to understand what a family is*

Trying to define what we mean when we use the word 'family' is not easy because there are so many different sorts of families in the world. For a bit of clarification though let's look into the Bible — it's always the right place to start.

Families as God intended

Husbands and wives

When God first placed human beings on the earth he put the first man (Adam) in a very special relationship with the first woman (Eve). Adam and Eve were not told just to be 'good friends' but to become lifelong committed partners, to stick to one another — through good times and bad. Ever since then, right at the heart of God's intention for family has always been a husband and wife united to one another in love.

Throughout the Bible it is clear that this relationship between husband and wife is to be specially prized and specially protected. Here are just a few Bible verses on the theme:

> (Husbands) ... be faithful to your own wife and give your love to her alone... So be happy with your wife and find your joy with the girl you married. *Proverbs 5:15,18*

> Every husband must love his wife as himself, and every wife must respect her husband. *Ephesians 5:33*

> Wives, submit to your husbands, for that is what
> you should do as Christians. Husbands, love your
> wives and do not be harsh with them. *Colossians
> 3:18,19*

So, right at the heart of God's intention for family is a wife and husband living together in love and commitment.

Children

It's God's intention that children should be born into a loving home where dads and mums live together in the way I've described. Right from the time that Adam and Eve were told to 'have many children' (Genesis 1:28), husbands and wives were expected to provide homes where their children could be protected from evil, provided for and where they could be taught to know and love God.

Jesus himself was born into a family where his dad and mum loved each other and where his parents' instruction helped him to grow up. This is what the Bible says:

> Jesus went back with [his parents] to Nazareth,
> where he was obedient to them… Jesus grew
> both in body and in wisdom, gaining favour with
> God and men. *Luke 2:51,52*

Parents should still give a high priority to their children, and children are told to pay special attention to what their parents tell them. All sorts of other people, like friends, teachers, rock stars or TV personalities will influence your life, but the Bible gives the key role to parents. Who pulls your strings? Here's God talking to you – yes, YOU – through the Bible.

> Children, it is your Christian duty to obey your
> parents, for this is the right thing to do.
>
> *Ephesians 6:1*

Now you can't get much plainer than that!

So right at the heart of 'family' in the Bible is mum and dad and their children. It's a really important group and no one and nothing should be allowed to split it up (until the children get old enough to leave home, of course!).

Other relations

In Bible times — and still in some parts of the world today — a family that just consisted of mum, dad and children would have been weird in the extreme. Also living in the family group there would have been other relatives such as grandparents or unmarried brothers, sisters — even nephews and nieces, aunts and uncles.

So our ideal biblical family isn't to be a little closed unit of mum, dad and their kids, but an open plan network of caring relationships that includes all relatives.

God's family

Jesus had some really radical things to say about family which show that there is a special family-type relationship which is to be enjoyed by *all* of his followers.

He was teaching in a house one day and Mary (his mum) and his brothers came to find him. They couldn't get into the house to see him because of the great crowds, so they sent in a messenger to tell him that they had arrived. Unexpectedly Jesus asked:

'Who is my mother? Who are my brothers?' He looked at the people sitting around him and said, 'Look! Here are my mother and brothers! Whoever does what God wants him to do is my brother, my sister, my mother.' *Mark 3:33–35*

Jesus was saying that God's family is bigger than just mum, dad, brothers and sisters. God's family is made up of everyone who loves him enough to obey him.

So in your church family you have all sorts of people: young, old, married, single, disabled, rich, poor etc. God loves them and has brought them – and you – into his family where the golden rule is 'Love one another'.

Friends and neighbours

God's plan for families was that they would not just exist for their own sake, but for the sake of others. Look at what he told Abram:

> I will give you many descendants, and they will become a great nation. I will bless you ... so that you will be a blessing. *Genesis 12:2,3*

Families-as-God-intended are supposed to be a blessing to others, to have 'open doors' to people that need help. God wants families today who are prepared to help people who need to experience the love and security of a family.

So, although in the Bible, 'family' starts with a very small number of people relating together in a very special and close way, it also widens out to include other relatives, all Christians and even friends and neighbours in need. This diagram may help explain God's family circles. You might like to write in names of people in each circle so that you can see who is in your 'biblical' family.

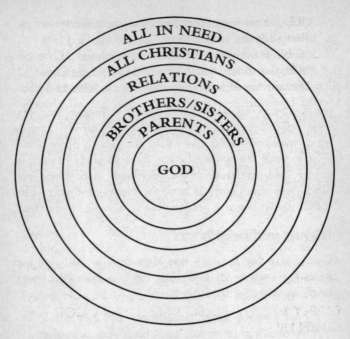

Circles from outer to inner: ALL IN NEED, ALL CHRISTIANS, RELATIONS, BROTHERS/SISTERS, PARENTS, GOD

Families as we know them!

Choose almost any family and you'll find a family that in some way doesn't fit God's ideal. A husband who has failed to love his wife – perhaps even gone off with another woman. A wife who has ignored her husband's feelings. A child who has disobeyed parents (unthinkable!). Relations who don't speak to each other. Churches where people are left isolated and alone.

Examples of families not getting it right are seemingly endless and if you're part of a family where things have gone wrong, you also know how hurtful it can all be. It's at this point that it's comforting to know that the Bible doesn't only tell us what families

SHOULD be like – it also gives us hope if our family has fallen short of God's ideal.

Many Bible families were less than perfect. One of the more dismal families in the Bible was King David's. King David himself was unfaithful to his wife and had a child by another woman, who was herself already married to one of King David's soldiers. David's son Amnon attacked his half-sister Tamar. His other son Absalom – Tamar's brother – then murdered Amnon in revenge. Later, Absalom plotted the overthrow of King David, his own father, forcing David to run from Jerusalem to save his life. Happy families – or what?

But despite all this pain and mess, the truly staggering thing is this. When God was looking around for a human family into which Jesus would be born, it was David's that he chose. Jesus was actually descended from King David! Whatever else this shows us, it makes one point very clearly, NO FAMILY HAS FAILED SO BADLY THAT GOD HAS GIVEN UP ON IT.

Whatever the shortcomings of your family, don't give up – keep working at making it better. The reason that God shows us in the Bible what a good family should be is not to make us feel guilty when ours messes up, but rather to show us what to work at to make ours better.

So, if Dad's gone and you're left on your own with Mum, then thank God for her and get stuck in to making family life as good as possible. If a new dad's come (complete with step-sister), then thank God for them and welcome them into the family. Respect them and care for them as best you can and pray for help to come to terms with all those churning emotions inside which sometimes spill over into anger and resentment. Try to talk about your feelings, not just bottle them up and try to spare a thought for how other people are feeling as well – it's hard for them too.

I'll write it again. Whatever the mess you might feel exists in your family GOD CAN WORK IN MESSED-UP FAMILIES. He has not given up on it, so make sure you don't either.

Outro

(What sort of family member are you?)

	Always	Often	Rarely	Never
1 I take my parent(s) into account when making decisions.	☐	☐	☐	☐
2 I keep in touch with other members of my family.	☐	☐	☐	☐
3 I treat the members of my church as 'family'.	☐	☐	☐	☐
4 I try to do my part to make family life a good experience.	☐	☐	☐	☐
5 I find it easy to accept that my brother/sister is different to me.	☐	☐	☐	☐
6 I make the effort to encourage my brother/sister.	☐	☐	☐	☐
7 I manage to stop myself saying things that wind up my brother/sister.	☐	☐	☐	☐
8 I quickly forgive my brother/sister when they've done something wrong.	☐	☐	☐	☐
9 I recognise that God has placed my parent(s) in authority over me.	☐	☐	☐	☐
10 I try to show my parent(s) God's love in the way I act at home.	☐	☐	☐	☐

	Always	Often	Rarely	Never
11 I pray for my parent(s).	☐	☐	☐	☐
12 I say sorry when I've been in the wrong.	☐	☐	☐	☐
13 I value the love that I get from my parent(s) more than the things they buy for me.	☐	☐	☐	☐
14 I believe that it is possible to be happy without having lots of 'things'.	☐	☐	☐	☐
15 I recognise that compared to millions of young people in the world I am incredibly well-off.	☐	☐	☐	☐
16 I am generous with my money and possessions.	☐	☐	☐	☐
17 I am willing to give up what I want to do to help out at home.	☐	☐	☐	☐
18 I volunteer to help before being asked or told what to do.	☐	☐	☐	☐
19 I remember to thank people who have served me.	☐	☐	☐	☐
20 Even when they don't deserve it...				
(a) I am ready to give my parents a second chance.	☐	☐	☐	☐
(b) I am able to be kind to my parents.	☐	☐	☐	☐
(c) I refuse to gossip about my parents' faults to others.	☐	☐	☐	☐
(d) I refuse to keep on bringing up my parent's(s') past failures.	☐	☐	☐	☐
21 I realise that when my parent(s) say 'No', they may have good reasons.	☐	☐	☐	☐

	Always	Often	Rarely	Never
22 I try to talk to my parents about the reasons why I want to do things.	☐	☐	☐	☐
23 I am willing to change my activities to take account of my parent's(s') wishes.	☐	☐	☐	☐
24 Even if I don't agree with their decision, I am trustworthy and don't go against my parent's(s') wishes when they're not looking.	☐	☐	☐	☐
25 I believe that I am a valuable person.	☐	☐	☐	☐
26 I believe that my life is useful.	☐	☐	☐	☐
27 I regularly look to the Bible to get a true idea of who I really am.	☐	☐	☐	☐
28 I refuse to behave badly just to get noticed.	☐	☐	☐	☐
29 If I have a disagreement with my parent(s), I try to talk it out with them.	☐	☐	☐	☐
30 I really try to understand my parent's(s') point of view.	☐	☐	☐	☐
31 I'm ready to suggest a number of different ways to solve a problem.	☐	☐	☐	☐
32 I refuse to sulk.	☐	☐	☐	☐
33 I am careful to choose the right moment to talk through big issues with my parent(s).	☐	☐	☐	☐
34 I take care to check that I am being understood.	☐	☐	☐	☐
35 I think carefully about the best way to say how I feel.	☐	☐	☐	☐

	Always	Often	Rarely	Never
36 I control my tongue.	☐	☐	☐	☐
37 I share my problems with a trusted, mature, older Christian.	☐	☐	☐	☐
38 When there's trouble at home I pray about it.	☐	☐	☐	☐
39 I understand that if my parent(s) are unkind to me it may be because of other pressures on their lives and nothing to do with me.	☐	☐	☐	☐
40 I put the top back on the toothpaste!	☐	☐	☐	☐

Scoring

So, how did you get on?

For every tick in the 'Always' column give yourself one point.

For every tick in the 'Often' column give yourself two points.

For every tick in the 'Rarely' column give yourself three points.

For every tick in the 'Never' column give yourself four points.

If you scored 43–63, you've got family life pretty well-sussed. Just watch out that you don't become big-headed about it – no one is perfect so there's always room for some improvement.

If you scored 64–106, you're doing pretty well, but there are a few areas where you need to get a bit of a grip. Start working on any areas where you scored three or four in the questionnaire.

If you scored 107–150, you've got quite a few problems at home and some of them at least are your fault! Have a look back through the book for some help in particular trouble areas.

If you scored above 150, then home life is probably a really painful experience for you and you need to seek help before things get completely unbearable for you and the people you live with. Find a Christian adult who you trust and feel you could talk to about your situation. Is there a youth leader at your church or a Christian teacher at school who you could speak to? Things can improve for you, but you need some guidance. So, find a guide and start sorting things out!

If you've enjoyed **KILLER PING-PONG**, here are some other books by David Lawrence you'll want to read…

The Expanded Chocolate Teapot

The classic guide to surviving as a Christian at school, including how (not) to start your new career at secondary school, and what to do when you feel you have let God down.

ISBN 1 85999 081 9
Price:£3.50

The Superglue Sandwich

If friends at school ask you 'Did God really make the world?' or 'Is the Bible really true?', what do you say? David Lawrence offers clues to the answers to these and other similar questions.

ISBN 0 86201 892 7
Price £3.50

Travels With My Zebra

The highly entertaining and readable story of Dave's travels with his zebra, written in the same classic style of *The Chocolate Teapot* and *The Superglue Sandwich*. Themes include: what to do when people let you down, choosing what to watch on TV, and how to spend your money, with pointers as to what the Bible has to say about it all.

ISBN 1 85999 262 5
Price £3.50

Available from your local Christian bookshop or from Scripture Union (Mail Order), PO Box 5148, Milton Keynes MLO, MK2 2YX
Phone: 01908 856006 **Fax**: 01908 856020
Email: subs@scriptureunion.org.uk
(P&p required for mail order. Please ask for details.)